The Secret and the Sacred Beacons

Brian S. Griffiths

*The Secret and Sacred within the
Brecon Beacons National Park*

ISBN: 0-86381-761-0

Line work: Brian S Griffiths
Cover design: Sian Parri
Photographs: Nick Jenkins

First published in 2001 by
Gwasg Carreg Gwalch, 12 Iard yr Orsaf, Llanrwst, Wales LL26 0EH
☎ 01492 642031   ✆ 01492 641502
✉ books@carreg-gwalch.co.uk   Web site: www.carreg-gwalch.co.uk

DEDICATION

To my dear wife Colleen

For her patience during my rambling,
in both body and mind.

Acknowledgements

With thanks to my friend, Peter Daley; fellow dreamer and hill walker. Without his help, his companionship and encouragement, this book might never have been written.

My thanks also to the following members of the Welsh National Museum, Cardiff:

Mark Lodwick for his help regarding the archaeological surveys at Waun Fignen Felen.

To Philip McDonald for his identification and classification of our finds at Llyn y Fan Fach.

Elizabeth Walker for her help and assistance concerning the finds within the Ogof Ffynnon Ddu Cave system.

To Dr Geraint Owen, Department of Geography at Swansea University, my appreciation for brief but impressive explanations of things geological.

My thanks to Peter Harvey of Rhayader for the background information regarding the discovery of human remains at Ogof Ffynnon Ddu.

Finally, my thanks to Nick Jenkins for providing me with some beautiful photographs of Castell Carreg Cennen and the lakes of Llyn y Fan Fach and Llyn y Fan Fawr.

Contents

Forward

It was with great pleasure that I received an invitation from Brian Griffiths to contribute a forward to this book. As part of our work in the Department Of Archaeology & Numismatics at the National Museums & Galleries of Wales, my colleagues and I identify and record a large number of objects found by members of the public. Amongst the most archaeologically important finds that have been reported in recent years were three worked flint blades which date to the Mesolithic, or Middle Stone Age, dates from c 8000 BC to c 3500 BC. It is the period of prehistory prior to the adoption of agriculture and pottery in which the inhabitants of the British Isles practised a peripatetic hunter-gatherer lifestyle. These are the first Mesolithic finds known from this site which at the time would have been a small lake in an area of extensive upland grazing. The flint blades from Llyn y Fan Fach presumably represent a hitherto unrecognised prehistoric occupational site. Their discovery contributes to our understanding of Mesolithic settlement and subsistence patterns in South Wales and also emphasises the important contribution that amateur researchers make to the understanding of our past. This book represents another major contribution in presenting the rich history and folklore of Wales to the public.

Philip Macdonald,
National Museums & Galleries of Wales.

Preface

Throughout the ages the mountains near my home have been the canvas upon which man has attempted to express a concept. They have long been the medium for the expression of complex ideas. Take the time to listen and the valleys, hills, slopes, lakes, and summits will give testimony to amazing tales of creation and evolution. Walk through dark valleys and deep gorges and they will tell of primitive life and early awakenings. A little higher, and the hills will speak of community and co-operation, of hearth and home, whilst the steeper slopes will speak of the longings, fears, praise and petitions of an ancient people. Visit the dark forbidding waters of the high lakes and they will give dreadful suspicions of ancient and terrible sacrifice and events executed by a naïve and fearful people. Make the journey to the peaks and summits and they will tell of sadness and death; yet, a death believed to be transformed by ritual into new and unknown beginnings.

What man has left in stone on these hills are the skeletal remains of his primitive life and death. Using the same landscape, he also expressed his infant evolution towards an absolute truth that is not found in the thing observed, but in the idea behind it: an idea that he, and we, currently call 'God'.

Introduction

Many people, especially those who have a love of the outdoors, will understand that sometimes, in a strange and inexplicable way, there is in the natural landscape a quality that can arouse undefinable emotional responses. It can simply be the arrangement of a heather filled rock outcrop or the way a stream falls from a rock ledge. It can be one of a hundred chance meetings with some aspect of the natural world, be it flora or fauna. Most of us can appreciate the natural beauty of a particular scene, and this same appreciation has inspired some of the worlds greatest artists. However, it is important to recognise that it is not always the subject that inspires, but often something within the subject. This might be the idea behind the theme – a certain quality within the observed that instantly activates a response within the observer.

I do not believe that these responses are the sole prerogative of the modern world or of a supposedly enlightened society, for I believe that people throughout those long ages of prehistory experienced them. Whatever it is in a landscape that attracts us would also have attracted our ancient ancestors, and whatever it is that inspires us would also have inspired them. Certainly, their motives and responses may have been considerably different and reflect different priorities. The cave paintings of hunting scenes that have been discovered at Lascaux in France illustrate this fact dramatically. However, to say that our early ancestors were only preoccupied with the business of living and dying would be an insult to their intellect and imagination. To deny them an appreciation of the wonder of the natural world is to deny our appreciation of the same, for it is an appreciation that has evolved from the same stock and lineage. The subjective quality is obvious and beauty it is said 'is in the eye of the beholder'.

Following this concept, my friend Peter Daley and I sought

to find the landscapes within our locality that attracted the people of prehistory. These landscapes have not only inspired generations of romantics and artists, but also provided the basic requirements of food and shelter for a primitive people. With this aim in mind, we set out to visit the remote, the lonely, the secret and the sacred.

My interest in these places has been fuelled over many years by what I have seen near my home, and in particular within the Brecon Beacons National Park. The geology of the central and western region of the park, unlike the old red sandstone summits to the east, consists of rocky outcrops of limestone, which terrace the hills and slopes. Here you will find deep gorges and wooded valleys where white waters spill in spectacular waterfalls. This combination of water and limestone has provided the park with some of its most valuable treasures – a vast subterranean world of caves and potholes which are already considered to be the largest and most impressive in the whole of Europe. Throughout the three separate sectors of the region you will also find some magnificent mountain peaks including Fan Brycheiniog at 802m, Corn Du at 873m, and Pen-y-fan at 886m.

As a child, the hills and caves of my locality were seen as the backdrop to mighty tales of King Arthur and his knights. Folklore tells how he lies with his companions in some rocky tomb, awaiting the call to arise and fight for the Welsh people. I was fascinated by these legends; an interest that was fuelled by tales of circles and cromlechs, witches and wizards. As if this were not enough to agitate a small boy's imagination, there were numerous stone structures scattered about the landscape which prompted some weird and wonderful tales! Following years of research and observation, many valid propositions have been submitted to explain these ancient sites. The result of these studies have contributed greatly to our understanding of the life and circumstances of the early inhabitants, and the findings have shed new light on the ancient people who populated our hills and valleys during those periods we classify as the Mesolithic, Neolithic, Bronze and Iron age. However, despite all that has been written, the fact remains that many of the conclusions regarding megalithic structures, standing stones and other features are little more than educated guesses. This is hardly surprising considering the scant evidence that exists. Indeed, there is very little to show purpose and meaning for the skeletal remains on our slopes and summits.

It is not the purpose of this book to explain these structures with any certainty, and neither can it be described as a serious work of academic interest. To present theories without the support of adequate evidence, however limited, is to invite scepticism and censure. Nevertheless, I would suggest that when we are dealing with areas outside the scope of the scientific, grounding our arguments on the solid bedrock of common sense, then the musings of the uneducated are as valid as those of the scholars and academics. Where science provides an absolute answer then let us acknowledge it. However; where science is unsure of itself, allow us our dreams.

With this in mind, and on behalf of the romantics amongst us, I lay claim to the rights of poets, priests, artists, and yes, even madmen who, over the centuries have coloured our history with offerings that have added life and dimension to the weary and well-worn pages of history. Where the experts take hold of the scientific, we reach for the abstract. Where they search for the material, we seek out the spiritual. Where they rejoice in the find, we glorify the spirit that created it.

Come then on a journey of discovery. Let us seek out evidence of our early ancestors, through their settlements, activity and ideas. But let us not confine ourselves to this alone. Let us search for the landscapes, and the structures that expressed those ideas of powers and principalities, of supplication and of sacrifice. But again, let us not stop there! Let us go beyond the ideas to the source of their inspiration. In so doing, we will discover the echoes and sensations of a naïve

10

people, a people whose spirituality was based on the sure knowledge of an omnipotent power that was, like ours, unknown, unseen, but experienced more fully than perhaps we could ever come to understand or appreciate.

Cwm Pwll-y-rhyd

Chapter One

In the Beginning

Throughout the centuries the mountains, hills and valleys of this island have seen immense changes as ice ages came and went. They have witnessed life's struggle to obtain a foothold as extremes of climate tested the very concept of life itself in a cruel game of survival. For millions of years the earth groaned and heaved as immense forces shaped this land, thrusting and heaving, splitting and slipping its way through alternate phases of creativity and destruction as new processes were tried, rejected, and reinvented.

I stood here twenty years ago and felt the same way then. Now I watch a friend go through the same emotions as he eagerly seeks a different vantage point in order to get a better view of this natural wonder. Standing there looking at this awe-inspiring sight, I realise that our landscape has much to offer those of us who need refreshment, be it physical or spiritual.

We are in the extremely narrow valley of Cwm Pwll-y-rhyd following a period of heavy rainfall, staring in disbelief as the upper reaches of Afon Nedd *(river Neath)* tumbles and tosses its foaming way towards us. Normally, by standing in the riverbed directly in front of such a raging mass, we would expect to be swept away by its awesome power. But here we are quite safe.

Directly between us and the torrent of water this ancient gorge seems to have split at right angles to the flow, leaving a deep fissure across the riverbed. Consequently, before reaching our vantage point, the water takes a sudden dive into the gap and, during the many centuries since the fissure was created, its action has cut through the limestone to form a new underground route. It eventually reappears some one hundred metres further downstream. The flow of water has continued to erode the existing riverbed, leaving the damp and abandoned

13

watercourse where we now stand considerably higher in elevation than the present river passage. It is an awesome experience to realise the time scale involved in this process.

Moving along through this old dry section, the thunderous roar of the waterfall is now replaced by an eerie silence. Maybe it is the high and narrow walls of the gorge. Perhaps it is the abrupt contrast of sound, but the roar of the water is now replaced by a silence that is broken only by the occasional plop of a water droplet from high above. As we move down into the ever-darkening chasm I begin to touch the primeval nature of this place; a place where evolution seems to have postponed its plans and gone off to do something else. What is left is a sad and empty canyon. Nevertheless, this old watercourse seems to generate a respectful sense of awe. With ever increasing wonder, we tentatively step our way into its dark depth.

Making our way downstream, we see that the floor consists of an impressive series of water smoothed limestone basins. These scooped out depressions are half filled with brackish water supplied not by the river, but through the benevolence of the vegetation and damp soil that crowns the high walls of this chasm. It seeps and dribbles from the rock faces to fill the natural basins at our feet. Progress can only be made by stepping from the lip of each of these algae-coated surfaces in tremulous hops and jumps.It is a manoeuvre that threatens to up end us at every step. As we make our tentative way downwards, the pungent smell of stagnation and rotting vegetation is everywhere.

Continuing downstream we are amazed to see the walls of this 'fossilised' waterway rubbed into smooth concave shapes, giving some idea of the previous energy and flow pattern of the water as it ripped, roared and surged its furious way through the rock, scouring and shaping the stone during a considerably more violent period of its history. These amazing surfaces provide an indication of how long the river flowed through here before its change of course. Stunted plant life peep out of dark clefts in the rock walls; ancient ferns, lichens and mosses are all straining their pale forms to catch what little light penetrates this damp and dark world. Here and there, dark 'windows' open into narrow passages that lead down to where the submerged river can be heard rampaging its underground route beneath our feet. Eventually we reach a point where the floor drops away. Peering over the ledge, we catch sight of the river emerging from a rock wall beneath us, to follow its ancient course downstream

Standing on the edge of this ancient and abandoned waterfall, I realise that we are viewing a scene frozen in time. No man had walked this landscape when the water shaped this ancient chasm. To look upon it now, still in its primeval state, fills one with an unbelievable sense of wonder.

In time, the glaciers of the Ice Age that once covered this place released their cold grip on the upland zones, and as the harsh conditions relented, new life forms began to seize the opportunities. In time, a new creature was seen on these hills; a creature that sought to control and take advantage of his surroundings through using the land and its habitat, and ultimately changing it, to provide for his needs. This man creature was still millions of years away, yet here in this place life was already striving to express itself in myriad types, colours and species, each one reaching a climax of expression in the variety and form of its fruits. Some say that without man, the spirit of God could not have walked through the land. Let them come here and wonder!

Grid Ref : SO 912137
Cwm Pwll-y-rhyd

Travelling along the A465 from Castell Nedd *(Neath)* towards Merthyr Tudful, turn off into the village of Glyn-nedd

(Glynneath). Whichever route you take into the village, you will eventually reach a set of traffic lights. At these lights, follow the signs for the little hamlet of Pontneddfechan. Following this unclassified road, you begin to climb the winding hill heading for Ystradfellte.

Soon the road begins to level out atop an area of common land with some fine views of a typical limestone landscape. There are dips and hollows, and the road follows these contours between gorse, heather and hawthorn. Eventually you will reach an open area where you may see several cars parked. This is a favourite spot for people who walk down to Afon Mellte to view some of the spectacular waterfalls. Nearby are a small shop and a public telephone. Continue onwards and. a short distance from here, you will see a narrow, well-surfaced road leading off to the left between some fields. Take this road.

Eventually the road passes in front of Berthlwyd Farm. A short distance from here the road surface begins to deteriorate and you will see a narrow track descend a short but steep incline on your left. Follow this track down and park on some rough ground at the bottom near 'Pont Pwll-y-rhyd.'

From here cross the stile into the wooded area and follow the river downstream to 'Cwm Pwll-y-rhyd.'

PWLL Y RHYD

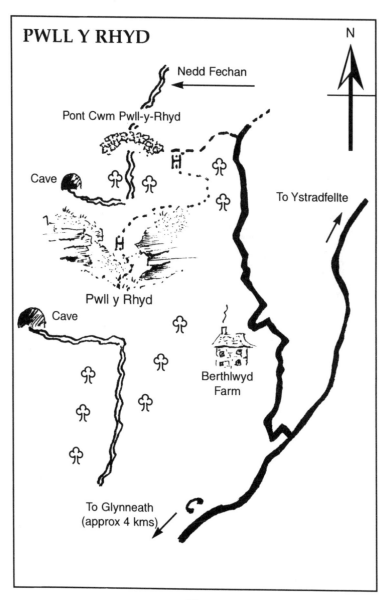

N

Nedd Fechan

Pont Cwm Pwll-y-Rhyd

Cave

To Ystradfellte

Pwll y Rhyd

Cave

Berthlwyd
Farm

To Glynneath
(approx 4 kms)

Waun Fignen Felen
The Yellow Bog
Circa 6000 B.C.
(An Impression)

Chapter Two

The Killing Fields

Let us now travel up Cwm Tawe *(valley)* to a point just beyond the 'Dan yr Ogof' show caves. Here we enter a deep sided valley to our left that was gouged by the movement of ice fields thousands of years previously. This rock and boulder strewn canyon provides the watercourse for the infant streams that drain the slopes of Fan Hir. We enter the narrow chasm a few hundred metres from its confluence with Afon Tawe. After checking our bearings, we head upstream, making a mental note of a location we might visit later; a feature marked on the map as 'Field System and Hut Circles'.

Let everyone beware, for Cwm Haffes is a desperate, knee jerking, ankle snapping and primeval watercourse. It is not for the faint footed or those of weak limbs. There is an easier route (see sketch plan) but then this is the route we must follow and as we will see later, for good reason.

Picking our way up the chasm, gingerly stepping from one boulder to another, the sense of the prehistoric presents itself in the jumble of rock and debris that litter the riverbed. During the arduous ascent through the narrow valley, I became immersed in the landscape. Soon we came upon enchanting water cascades that cut deeply into the bedrock. Mountain ash and heather cling precariously from the side walls of the canyon, their shoots bathed in damp moisture filtered from wind-blown clouds of spray. Reaching a convenient slab of rock, we take the opportunity to rest. Breathlessly, I scan the area below. Apart from a few gnarled and weathered hawthorns, their twisted form reinforcing the sense of the aged and ancient, the tree cover is sparse. Here and there, spongy black peat break through the late winter brown, with saturated marshland that is threatening to the unwary. Sitting here with the river bed below, I muse on recent archaeological investigations carried out at an area of peat bog a short distance to the west of where we sit. This peat bog, known as Waun Fignen Felen, provided us with new insights into our prehistoric ancestors.

You could pass Waun Fignen Felen and express nothing more than mild interest. Lying at an altitude of 485m there is nothing to suggest its primitive origins other than a deeply eroded expanse of blanket peat. The only notable feature within close proximity is a large swallow hole and, at its eastern extremity, the deeply cut watercourse of Cwm Haffes where we now sit. Approaching the area from the west, the black peat that constitutes Waun Fignen Felen is seen as a dark stain on the landscape. This area of marsh is set within a shallow depression and, despite its altitude, is surrounded by higher ground. To the north the spectacular Fan Brycheiniog stands in majestic prominence. Lying as it does in a natural basin, the bog remains concealed from lower levels; a situation, which we will see, which was to become significant.

To the casual hill walker, there is nothing to suggest that this bog is anything special. However, during the period 1979 to 1984, and again in 1992, following field studies, a number of important finds of Mesolithic origin were made at Waun Fignen Felen. These included flint flakes, blades, scrapers, a drilled stone bead, a barbed and tanged arrowhead and other primitive artefacts. Almost all of these finds were discovered within the mineral sediments beneath the peat, and from surface scatters around its edge. The finds suggested that people had visited this site during several phases covering the Mesolithic, (8000-6,000BC) Neolithic, (6000-3000BC) and Bronze age, (3000-2,500BC). In addition, archaeologists uncovered an amount of waste material near the edge of the bog, which indicated the use and reworking of primitive hunting tools, because the discarded stone chips gave evidence of flint *knapping*. Most of these finds were discovered at the east and north-eastern section, with very few artefacts being retrieved elsewhere.

Following these impressive investigations, it was shown that this expanse of peat bog was once a shallow lake covering an area roughly 300m by 200m. Evidence from core samples suggest that, by the time people of the Mesolithic Age first ventured into these mountains, the lake had become partly overgrown with reeds, and probably contained only seasonal standing water. There is also evidence of the presence of woodland, provided by the discovery of pollen samples of birch, hazel, and elm. During the period 8,000BC to about 4,000BC, the reed swamp vegetation continued to infill the lake, whilst the blanket peat probably blocked the outlets from the basin and was responsible for its subsequent infilling. At around 2,000BC, the lake perimeter and upland slopes were eventually denuded of tree cover, leading to the development of fully open conditions.

Until fairly recently, there was very little evidence that Mesolithic people used upland sites in south Wales. However, the recent finds have shed new evidence to support the movements and activities of these people within the Western Sector of the National Park. But why were they here? What were they doing? Why should almost all of the recovered specimens of hunting tools, blades, arrowheads, microliths, points, etc. be found almost without exception at the northern edge of Waun Fignen Felen, and what is the relevance of these finds to this ancient lake. An impressive paper: *Mynydd Du and Fforest Fawr: The Evolution of an Upland Landscape*, published by the Royal Commission Ancient and Historical Monuments in Wales, provides answers to some of these questions. However, in order to appreciate these findings we must apply a little imagination. To do this we must first travel back in time; a time when the climate and conditions were very different. To appreciate the motives of the people who came to Waun Fignen Felen we will follow their route to the lake; hence the reason why we now find ourselves sitting amongst the rugged terrain that is Cwm Haffes. In this moment of relaxed reverie, the reality of ancient events gradually takes shape.

They enter the gorge from near its confluence with Afon Tawe. Lean, athletic young men wearing hide trews, some are bare chested whilst others wear hide tunics, but all wear moccasin style footwear. Bulging leather pouches hang heavily from their torsos, and each man carries several wooden shafted spears and spear throwers, some of bone and others of reindeer and elk antler. It is obvious that each item is a proud possession, lavishly decorated with carvings and colours that represents the shape and form of animals and birds. Despite their load, they still move with a grace and athleticism that tells of expertise, experience and purpose. This is a Mesolithic hunting party.

Their softly clad feet leaping surely and silently from boulder to boulder, they meander up through the narrow gorge in single file. A few yards above the west wall of this deep valley lies their objective, for they are heading towards the still waters of a reed filled upland lake.

Reaching Sgwd Ddu, a small waterfall, the group pause and check their weaponry. One or two reach into their pouches and remove some large flint pebbles that are carefully examined before being returned to the bag. These are stock material from which replacement barbs, blades, and spear tips will be fashioned should the need arise.

They reach this point in their journey without any words being exchanged. Not a sound has been made that will have alerted the animals grazing at the edge of the lake. Some in this hunting party have travelled many miles to seek out this traditional hunting ground, but others will have spent several months in the shelter provided by the caves of Dan yr Ogof. Now gathering themselves together, they carefully prepare for the final part of their journey. With gestures and signals, the group scales the left-hand side of Sgwd Ddu that opens out into the higher reaches of the 'Cwm,' and then head ever upwards.

The group purposefully makes its way through the gorge ahead. Suddenly, one youth leaves the group and, placing his weapon on the ground, quickly scales the steep slope of the left flank. On reaching the top he spread-eagles himself atop the crest to scan the landscape ahead. He then signals to the others before descending the slope and rejoining the group. Together again, they make progress up the valley.

During spring and summer, wild duck, waterfowl, and other marsh birds flock here, whilst moose, elk, reindeer, wild boar and red deer graze and drink at various times and seasons around the perimeter of this upland lake. Lying as it does within westerly moving airstreams, the hunting party's approach from the east through Cwm Haffes has ensured that any game within the vicinity of the lake will not pick up their scent. They exit the valley at the north-eastern shoreline, upwind of the lake basin, having ensured that the animals remain oblivious of their presence. The group then splits into three, the main body taking the centre whilst the others take up position on the left and right flanks. In tense and excited anticipation, they reach a point where the deeply incised valley gradually rises to level ground. They get their first glimpse of the lake, and with it the sight of their prey.

Making use of the cover provided by the hazel, birch, and low growing vegetation, the hunters are able to stalk their prey to within a few metres, maintaining a low profile until they find the range and position for a first strike. Engaging the spear throwers into the notches on the spear shafts, they quickly rise to a standing position and hurl their missiles. The spears find their targets with deadly accuracy.

Turning in terror and confusion, the animals on the opposite bank, the one facing the hunters, bolt from the lake edge to the safety of the higher slopes. But for those on the eastern shoreline, alerted by the panic on the opposite shore, the escape route is limited. In blind panic, the ambushed animals *turn and twist, dart and jink to avoid the hunters who seem to be everywhere. The only alternative is the lake itself and some hurl themselves into the water in a vain attempt to reach safety. With forward movement restricted by water and reeds, the mad dash to freedom is cruelly ended in a hail of spears. Shouts of triumph and bleats of panic continue to break the tranquillity as mayhem and madness fill the lake basin.*

Following the kill, the hunters carry out instant and necessary maintenance on weapons, replacing spear tips and blades. The routine tasks completed, all hands will be turned to butchering so as to prepare the meat for transport back to the community. Eventually the hunters leave, and peace and tranquillity once again comes to reign.

Perhaps the hunters lit a fire close to a nearby pool and prepared or consumed a little of the kill here. Some distance from the north-western shoreline is a pool of water known in Welsh as 'Pwll-y-cig' *(the flesh pool)*. A little further to the south-west you will find a place called 'Cwm Twrch' *(the valley of the hog or boar)*. Is it possible that the echoes of a long forgotten time and environment reverberate still in these mountains in the place names?

Abandoning wild speculation, we make a cursory search of the area. Like excited children we stop at every weather-worn patch of peat to examine stone and pebble until our eyes begin to water. Knowing that the area had previously been minutely examined by archaeologists, there seems to be very little likelihood of us finding anything to support the theory. After about two hours of fruitless searching, I begin to wonder if we should abandon our efforts when, suddenly, my eye catches a tiny sliver of stone protruding from the top of an eroded peat mound. Picking it up I soon realise that what I am holding is a razor sharp flint blade; a blade that might have been first crafted at this spot some eight to ten thousand years previously. Knowing that there is not a great quantity of naturally occurring flint deposits, if indeed any, in this area, the find suggests that it was brought here.

Whoever fashioned these implements once stood where we now stand. Processions of people in the ensuing millennia have come to this place and even though time and space separate us, I feel a connection. In these first moments of discovery those ancient people and I stand united; both of us transcending time; both of us representing man's evolutionary journey through the ages; through worlds both physical and spiritual.

Grid Ref: SN 822181 & SN 835173
The Killing Fields

Take the A4067 road between Swansea *(Abertawe)* and Brecon, *(Aberhonddu)* making for the 'Dan yr Ogof' show caves. A few hundred metres on the Brecon side of the entrance to the Cave complex, there is a stile. Cross the stile and follow the footpath up through the farmyard. Soon you will cross a second stile that leads into Cwm Haffes. From here you can choose to either follow the course of the river upstream, or cross the river bed just beyond the stile, and follow the path that ascends the slopes of the left-hand side of the river. If you choose the second option, make sure you use map and compass, as the path is not always clearly marked. Eventually you will reach Waun Fignen Felen, which is unmistakable due to its expanse of blanket peat.

CWM HAFFES & WAUN FIGNEN FELEN

Waun Fignen Felen

Afon Haffes

Cwm Haffes

Dan yr Ogof
Showcaves

To Brecon

A4067

To Swansea

Afon Tawe

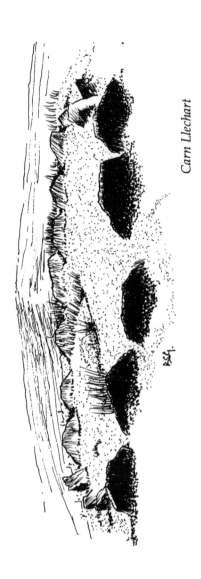

Carn Llechart

Chapter Three

Sacred Cemeteries

With boyhood friends, I fought many a summers campaign on the hills overlooking my home. *The Battle of the Little Big Horn, Rourkes Drift, The Alamo*, several skirmishes involving Red Indians, German infantry, Japanese jungle fighters and even aliens from far-flung galaxies – they all fought on these slopes! During a frontal attack involving any one of these ruthless foes, I would take cover behind some nearby lump in the landscape and pick off the enemy at leisure as they advanced through the low growing heather. Little did I realise that these insignificant mounds predated my epic battles by thousands of years. If I had known of the primordial nature of my surroundings, I belive my interest in these tussock-covered mounds would have been less strategic, and far more speculative.

Not too far from where I fought my battles, there was another forsaken and forgotten curiosity. However, this one could claim celebrity status, the late and eminent Prof. Mortimer Wheeler being one of several to have commented upon it. High upon the slopes overlooking the upper reaches of Afon Clydach, at a point above and to the north-west of the town of Pontardawe, is a site that is described on the Ordnance Survey map as 'Remains of burial chamber'. Following a rough track, it is a leisurely climb to the crest of the hill where this supposed burial chamber is located. Behind and below, the valley road runs between Pontardawe and Ammanford and in the far distance, marking the north-eastern boundary between south and mid Wales, are the exposed slopes of Y Mynydd Du *(The Black Mountain)*. Many get confused between this and Y Mynyddoedd Duon *(The Black Mountains)*, but those can be found to the east of the A470 from Brecon to Merthyr.

Turning my attention back to Mynydd Carn Llechart, which is our immediate surrounding, I am instantly conscious of the bleakness of this place. Maybe it is the chill breeze or the greyness of the day. It may be the knowledge of what lies beneath my feet. Perhaps it is the anticipation of finding what I am searching for that perturbs and unsettles me, but I am instantly conscious of a strange, disconcerting sorrow that pervades this landscape. Normally anything connected with prehistory generates eager interest. This time, my eagerness is tempered by a disturbing sense of melancholy. All around there is an emptiness which has nothing to do with the barren mountain itself for it originates at a deeper, more substantial level. With a mixture of emotions we head for a point that offers a better view of our surroundings.

I very nearly miss it, but my companion's shout attracts my attention. Turning, I see him standing above an arrangement of rocks. Walking back, I come to realise that the anonymous jumble of stone slabs lying in disarray at his feet are the age-old remnants of a Neolithic burial site! Our excitement mounts as we peer and poke, touch and ponder our way around these remarkable remains. Standing on a recumbent slab of rock, we attempt to make some sense of this haphazard assortment of stone.

This tomb is one of thirteen 'Chambered Tombs' recorded in Morgannwg *(the County of Glamorgan)*. Generally they are found in lower areas, but this one at Mynydd Carn Llechart is very much in the upland region of the county. They are the most common evidence of a period in history known as the Late Neolithic Age, an era that in this part of Wales is generally regarded to have taken place sometime around 4000BC. Normally, such structures as these are composed of a stone lined chamber, or chambers, covered with a mound of earth, all enclosed and retained by a walling of local stone. These tombs can be quite extensive, and contain passages as well as any number of associated chambers. The despoiled condition of this site, and the lack of any evidence of a previous covering mound makes interpretation of its original construction and layout difficult. Not only has it suffered at the hands of grave robbers, it is also suggested that some of the original material may have been removed by the later 'Bronze Age' people, to provide material for constructing some sixteen to twenty other burial sites that have been identified atop this mountain ridge!

Leaving the remnants of this ancient chambered tomb, we move across the top of the ridge to be suddenly confronted by a bizarre circle of twenty-five stone slabs that open out from the ground like the petals of some huge flower. I have seen many cairns in the past, usually consisting of a mound of stone piled on a slope or summit, but this is different. This one has a presence about it and, more dramatically, the central burial cist which it enclosed, although despoiled, lies exposed and partially intact. In a rush of boyish excitement I hastily step into the circle to explore this mystery. But I am immediately brought to a halt. My disrespectful behaviour is reprimanded by a sudden and unassailable sense that comes of treading on sacred soil.

This Bronze Age construction is typical of the period, for it was an extension of what had gone before. It was the practice of the 'Neolithic' or 'New Stone Age' people to bury their dead in large chambered tombs. However, the Bronze Age community abandoned this practice, choosing to inter the remains individually within a generally smaller construction. Another departure was the change from inhumation to cremation, with the ashes of the deceased being placed in a pottery urn and set within a central stone clad cist, sealed by a small capstone. The entire structure would then have been overlaid by suitable material. Where these burials occurred on the higher slopes and summits, they were usually covered with stones and referred to as 'Cairns'. Those constructed in the lower valleys were usually of earth, and described as 'Barrows'. All of these structures, so typical of the Bronze Age, are thought to date from the 2nd millennium BC.

The people who built these cairns and barrows are referred to as the 'Beaker People', the name taken from the distinctive style of pottery that they used to contain their cremated remains. There are many different types of cairn to be found within South Wales; some large, some small, some edged with a kerb of stone, others with revetment walling; others are surrounded by a bank and some by a ditch. This one is of a different type, but nevertheless quite common, and known as a ring cairn. The central pit was a small rectangular excavation lined on three sides by stone slabs. The fourth slab, and the capstone, which would have completed the total sealing of the small chamber, were missing, having been desecrated some time previously. Standing above this open grave, you sense the ancient people who came to these slopes for their presence still haunts this mountain.

In such a place and moment as this, the present slips easily into the past. The meaning and purpose of the area slowly unfolds in all its bleak, yet sacred, history. This is not just another pile of anonymous stones; some minor archaeological interest. This was the final resting place of a living personality who possessed feelings and emotions and was a member of my community. He, or she, lived and walked these hills some four to five thousand years before me, but I was conscious that the people who populated these hills were my ancestral stock.

The sanctity of this place is immediately reinforced when I lift my head and look back at the remains of the chambered tomb we had left earlier. I am suddenly aware of the continuity that is enshrined on this mountain, and in these stones. Whilst these two structures are linked by location and intent, and only yards apart, they are in fact separated by over a thousand years in time and culture, emphasising the antiquity and sacred nature of Mynydd Carn Llechart. From the evidence of this desolate hillside we must assume that ritualistic inhumation and cremation was practiced here over a period covering both the Neolithic and Bronze age. Here on this mountain, we have proof of a continuity of purpose that far exceeds anything seen in the contemporary world. Although the tombs are abandoned now, there is one aspect of their culture that still survives, albeit in diminished form, and that is their concept of life beyond death.

The belief in an afterlife and the continuity of the individual in a state beyond death preceded the Christian doctrine by many thousands of years, and was a principle amply demonstrated by the number and quality of grave goods that have been found accompanying both Neolithic and Bronze Age burial. The earliest example from my locality is the famous 'Red Lady of Paviland' who, incidentally, was not a lady but the skeletal remains of a young man. The Revd William Buckland, Professor of Geology at Oxford, found the remains in a sea cave on the Gower Peninsula in 1823. They were covered in red ochre, and were accompanied by what are assumed were personal effects of the dead man; some small shells and fragments of about forty to fifty ivory rods, varying between one to four inches (2.5-10cm) in length. Subsequent analysis suggests that this inhumation was dated to around 24,000BC, making it one of, if not the earliest example of primitive burial to be found in south Wales.

Death came in many different guises in the hostile and dangerous world of our ancestors, whether swiftly at the hands of a foe or an enraged and hungry predator, or more subtly through the creeping decay of age or disease. Yet despite the hopelessness generated by the experience; despite its apparent finality, the people were already committed to the idea of individual survival. This belief in an afterlife was a theme that preoccupied our ancestors from their earliest emergence. Nevertheless, the thread that runs through the ages is not the practices they employed to deal with death. It is, rather, the spirituality that drove it – a spiritual concept that has been traced through different cultures, societies and ages right up to this present day.

If we look upon this hillside and its stone edifices as just some primitive expression of burial custom and practice, we miss the greater and more significant aspect of the human condition that this mountain and these constructions underpin. This is not just some convenient patch of wasteland or a primitive crematorium. No, this mountain was the focus for a ritual act, the origins of which took root when man first took his first faltering and fearful steps out of the undergrowth into the light. It began from the moment his desire to take, dominate, and control was replaced by loving relationships based on the principle of self sacrifice, as opposed to self will. Unlike his Neanderthal ancestors who would walk away from grief and continue the business of surviving, our newly thinking cousin, when faced with the loss of a partner or fellow member of the community, would begin to question the pain. In those moments; in that very first act of questioning, he was wrenched from a world of cause and effect and plunged into a new order. From now on he would come to experience new ideas; abandoning his primitive ignorance to begin the quest for the truth of his condition. In that first defining moment, when death was questioned, death's silence hinted at something greater and more powerful than death itself. Later his search would be expressed in the way his ideas were reflected in the landscape, and the first of these desperate infant cries are expressed within the structures found on this sad and lonely windswept hill.

It is a poignant experience to stand here and reflect on childhood memories in the knowledge that most of the people who were part of those memories no longer shared my life. Once again, I relived boyhood adventures and expeditions to these hills, when shared bottles of pop would wash down hastily prepared bread and jam sandwiches. Memories of joyous Sunday afternoon family picnics were recalled, all encompassed within the warmth of what seemed to be an eternal summer. Standing here, recalling those memories of friends and family, I know with an almost experiential certainty that, in the course of remembering them on this summit, they live on at some other level of being and experience.

Grid Ref: SN 696063
Sacred Cemeteries

Take the A4067 to Pontardawe, and head for the centre of the village. At the traffic lights, take the A474 towards Ammanford. Approximately one mile (1.6km) from Pontardawe, at the village of Rhyd-y-fro, you will see 'The Travellers Rest,' pub on your right. The road dips here and, at the bottom of the hill, take the unclassified road on your left which crosses over a narrow bridge. From this point, the road begins to climb. Continue upwards until you cross a cattle grid. Just beyond the grid is a rough roadway on your left. Follow this up as it bends around. Do not follow it to the farm but continue on, following the track that skirts along the field boundary walls along the top of the ridge. Soon the track turns left. Follow it and, when you reach the crest, stop and strike out across the moorland on your right where you will find 'Carn Llechart'. After viewing this ring cairn, turn westward and descend the slopes a little to where you will come across the remains of a Neolithic burial chamber.

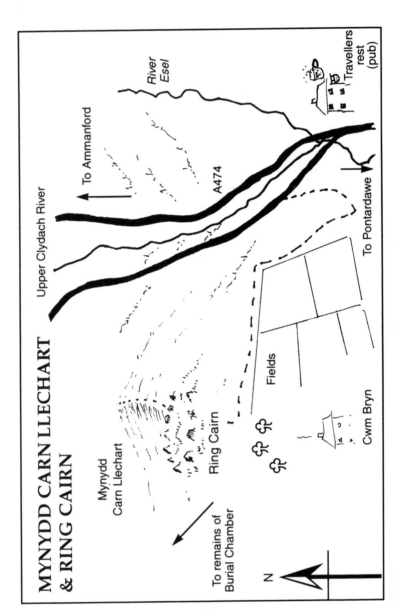

MYNYDD CARN LLECHART & RING CAIRN

River Esel

Travellers rest (pub)

To Ammanford

A474

Upper Clydach River

To Pontardawe

Fields

Cwm Bryn

Mynydd Carn Llechart

Ring Cairn

To remains of Burial Chamber

N

Maen Llia

Chapter Four

The Megalith

The artefacts and antiquities in my backyard do not seem to attract the attention that is reserved for more celebrated locations such as Stonehenge and Avebury. Perhaps our geography and relative isolation in this modern age are the reasons. Neither are they as dramatic, but still, there are many theories connected to them to explain their presence in our ancient and mysterious landscape. However, despite all the conjecture and opinions, the standing stones, circles, ellipsis, barrows, avenues, pillow mounds, ditches and countless other strange signatures on our hills have never, as yet, been satisfactorily explained. Regardless of our seemingly arrogant knowledge of past, present and future, the simple statements enshrined in these ancient structures continue to evade us. They remain an entertaining enigma!

So join me now, and let us visit a celebrated icon that has stood sentinel in these hills for far longer than history can testify. Travelling up the narrow road from the tiny village of Ystradfellte, we follow Afon Llia towards its source, until we come upon an engaging mystery, an impressive sixteen-tonne standing stone known as 'Maen Llia'. The name commonly attributed to standing stones is *Menhir*. The word is a corruption of the ancient Welsh term *Maen Hir*, inasmuch as the Welsh word *Maen* means 'stone', whilst *Hir* is translated to 'long'. In time, *Maen Hir* was corrupted to *Menhir*, a word that has become universal throughout Western Europe when describing such monoliths.

This impressive example stands in magnificent isolation at the head of Cwm Llia *(valley)* and, due to its location, is one of very few that may be examined without trekking across remote hills and moorland. Without any firm evidence, everyone seems to have a personal theory as to the purpose of such massive structures. Suggestions have included centres of earth energy, foci for healing, tribal monuments, primitive astronomical instruments, seasonal calendars, memorial stones for long dead heroes, religious icons, ritual sites, sacrificial stones, and even guidance beacons for flying saucers! Although many of these propositions may be viewed as being a little outlandish, somewhere in there, the truth abides. There is, however, a consensus amongst experts that this stone is probably a route marker; a primitive aid to navigation. Whilst that description can quite easily be applied to other similar standing stones within the Brecon Beacons National Park, I feel that Maen Llia is a bit special. Most standing stones come with a little bit of folklore attached, and Maen Llia is no exception. It is said that on certain nights it gets up and ambles down to the nearby stream for a drink! As in most folklore, it is difficult to disentangle fact from fantasy when the truth is invariably corrupted and disseminated by generations of imaginative storytellers. However, it is interesting that this theme of stone and water is not only found within this National Park, but is applied to monoliths found in other parts of the country. As many of these stones are found near the source of a river, lakes or other water sites, it seems to indicate a correlation between the two. Sometimes, through a process of extrapolation, you can arrive at the root cause of an idea or action, charting its history back through the centuries to its origins in other distant places and other ancient histories. When you recall this stone's need for its nightly drink, consider this ancient text written about 1800BC.

'And God said unto him (Jacob), I am God Almighty: be fruitful and multiply; a nation and a company of nations shall be thee, and Kings shall come out of thy loins;

and the land which I gave Abraham and Isaac, too I will give it, and to thy seed after thee will I give the land.

And God went up from him in the place where he talked with him. And Jacob set up a pillar in the place where he talked with him, **even a pillar of stone**: *and he poured a* **drink** *offering thereon, and he poured oil thereon.'* (Genesis: Chapter 35. Verse 11-14.)

Earlier I explained how the original *Menhir* in the Welsh language meant 'Long Stone'. There is, however, a Welsh word that is beyond literal translation, but defines an important part of our culture. Over the centuries this word has come to represent far more than its literal meaning, for it is *'Hiraeth'*. Many attempts have been made to translate the word, but the closest that one can get, and the ones that most agree upon, are a combination of 'soul feeling' and 'unexplainable longing'. And there are those who will try to tell you that the word *Menhir* is really the corrupt form of *Maen Hiraeth* rather than *Maen Hir*.

Standing on this high, windswept ridge, something inside me acknowledges the truth of that argument. For me, this giant monolith is primitive man's attempts to express his longing. Every day of his often difficult and dangerous existence, he witnessed a creative power that ordered the sun, the moon, the stars and the seasons. These forces affected his daily life to an extent that we, in our more sophisticated world, could never come to appreciate. Driven by a basic spiritual sense of awe and wonder, he expressed his longing in the only way he felt capable: to reach up and communicate. Just as the tall spires of our churches reach up in subconscious longing, so too did our primitive ancestors raise this stone in a desire to grasp their god. Enveloped in the shadow of this mighty stone I am conscious of the fact that I echo the sensations of hundreds of other people, who down the centuries have stood on this very same spot, thinking the same thoughts and feeling the same feelings.

On a cold, wet and miserable November afternoon, with the

mist and low cloud clinging to my face, I gaze up at this huge diamond shaped slab, desperately trying to understand. Sited as it is on a lonely windswept mountain, I see no practical reason why anyone should want to go the effort of raising such an enormous weight into a vertical position. The people who undertook this laborious and somewhat dangerous task were primitive tribal folk. Living was difficult enough without risking life and limb on such a hazardous and time-consuming task. To regard this stone as simply a marker, or primitive signpost in order to aid navigation is to do an injustice to both the priorities and sensibilities of these people. Surely, other lighter and more easily manageable stones found nearby would have been selected for so mundane a purpose? No, this effort was in answer to a greater and nobler need. It was a need to appease, to praise, to share and, more importantly, to communicate with something or someone greater than themselves. Standing here now, I am aware of a haunting presence that pervades the area. Immersed in the mood of this mountain, I make my clumsy, uncomfortable way forward in a tentative, self-conscious movement. As I approach I feel threatened beneath its towering bulk, and yet I stretch out a trembling, anticipatory hand, in an unexplainable need to bridge the centuries.

Here on this lonely moor, some two thousand feet (610m) above sea level, a large group of men dressed in rough clothing are gathered around the stone, some seated, some standing, but all exhausted by the effort they have made. Now it is done they stare in awe at what they have achieved. The raising of this monolith marks an inspirational step into intellectual and spiritual advancement. It signals a departure from reacting to their needs, to expressing them. For our ancestors, this was also a leap in cultural and artistic expression. But then this was not art for arts sake. How often have we in the modern age longed to communicate a thought, idea or principle, but failed because all the mediums available were inadequate. How often have we longed for the skill of the artist or musician who, through the use of art, brings out something from within himself that is beyond mere words or images? And then in a symphony of sound, in a rush of words or in the strokes of a brush, he gives witness to an idea. He expresses abstract truths that resonate deeply in the spirit, creating new heights of awareness and providing the observer with subtle glimpses of new realities. So it is with this stone. This is no simple route marker! This is a 'stone of longing', but it is also a witness to mankind's first grasp at a truth that had stirred, but yet evaded him. Do we not still try to follow his example in our stumbling steps into self-expression?

> *'And the people said unto Joshua, "The LORD our God will we serve, and his voice we will obey."*
>
> *So Joshua made a covenant with the people that day, and set them a statute and an ordinance in Shechem.*
>
> *And Joshua wrote these words in the book of the law of God,* **and took a great stone, and set it up there under an oak,** *that was by the sanctuary of the Lord.*
>
> *And Joshua said unto all the people,* **'Behold, this stone shall be a witness unto us; for it hath heard all the words of the Lord which he spake unto us: it shall be therefore a witness unto you, lest ye deny your God.'**
> (Joshua: Chapter 24. Verses 24-27.)

Grid Ref: SO 924192
The Megalith

From Ystradfellte, follow Afon Llia upstream along the unclassified valley road towards Pontsenni *(Sennybridge)* and Aberhonddu *(Brecon)*. On reaching the head of the valley, you will see Maen Llia a few metres off to your right. Cross the stile at the side of the road to view it at close quarters.

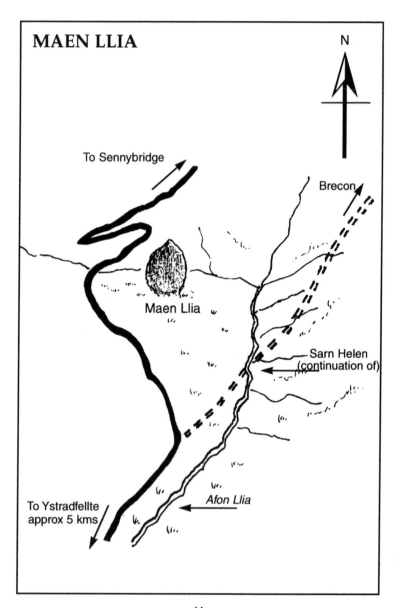

MAEN LLIA

N

To Sennybridge

Brecon

Maen Llia

Sarn Helen
(continuation of)

To Ystradfellte
approx 5 kms

Afon Llia

Saith Maen

Chapter Five

Saith Maen

High in the upper reaches of Cwm Tawe *(the Swansea Valley)* there is a place that has attracted people for at least ten thousand years! Y Mynydd Du *(The Black Mountain)* provides little evidence to suggest such ancient pre-occupation. Certainly, there is ample indication of the exploitation of mineral deposits, which is mainly restricted to the past two or three centuries, but there is little evidence of activity that predates this period.

Today, people are attracted here by the wild beauty. However, to present this wonder as some popular tourist trap is to diminish its ancient significance and inherent mystique. In order to understand these heights, we must follow ancient footprints, see through ancient eyes and approach this landscape in the spirit of the people who first defined the special character of this place. This will involve us in a journey consisting of two elements; the rudiments of which will give us some appreciation of the truth of this special location. The first part of our journey involves a physical trek, travelling to our destination via the hunting grounds and homesteads of our ancestors. The second is of a different kind and will call upon our senses and imagination. So let us begin by taking the road to Craig-y-nos.

Lest any one reading this book fail to understand our preoccupation with the romantic, let them come here to Glyntawe high in the Swansea valley. Here they will find that others tapped into the mood of these mountains long before us. What more romantic a name than 'Craig-y-nos' *(rock of the night)* could be bestowed upon this castle that sits alongside the main Swansea to Brecon road, near the Dan yr Ogof show caves. This impressive building was the home of Madame Adelina Patti, international diva of the opera, darling of millions and special favourite of Prince Edward VII.

The chill air of mid-April is surprising, snapping at legs as we get out of the car and sending me rummaging for windproofs and an extra sweater. It may be early spring but here, in the foothills of the Brecon Beacons, the seasons are always that little bit unsure of themselves. But despite the low temperature, the conditions are perfect with mountain ridges set upon a blue sky and still air. Drifts of late lying snow cling to the mountaintops in defiant isolation, but they are few and already retreating from the strengthening sunshine. Our steep climb takes us up Cribarth and, having ascended this steep limestone crag, we head for an alignment of stones known as 'Saith Maen' *(seven stones)*. The name in itself describes what we might expect to see. But on these mountains, expectations are often ambushed by the unexpected and senses can be confounded by the senseless.

This sector of the park is characterised by weather worn rock outcrops, holes and ancient mysteries. At every mound, ditch, hollow and earthwork, the ghosts of a primitive people constantly clamour for attention, all within a terrain akin to some lunar landscape. Eventually however we arrive atop a small level plateau and stand before the mystery of Saith Maen.

Yes, there are undoubtedly seven stones here. Of the seven, five are still upright and earth-fast, whilst two others lie nearby. One of the two recumbent stones is largest of all, measuring some 2.9m in length, whilst those that remain upright reach a maximum height of 1.7m. In other parts of the country where similar alignments have been noted, they are usually connected to some ancient feature. However, in this instance expert opinion suggests that Saith Maen is not associated with any other monuments of the period. Neither is there any evidence to connect these stones with anything else in the locality, and nothing to suggest their purpose or intent.

Arriving at this spot after such an arduous climb, the first

The ancient limestone walls of Cwm Pwll y Rhyd.

The ring cairn on mynydd Carnllechart.

Peter Daley examining the central cist of the ring cairn.

Peter examining the possible 'capstone' of a neolithic burial chamber on mynydd Carnllechart.

The ring cairn on mynydd Carnllechart.

The enigatic Saith Maen.

The human remains found in Ogof Ffynnon Ddu in 1946
The Greedy Farmer. (Photo: Peter Harvey)

Water cascades on Cwm Haffes.

Peter Daley at the base of Sgwyd Ddu.

Water cascades on Cwm Haffes.

Maen Llia.

'Saith Maen' looking towards Cwm Haffes and Fan Hir.

Maen Mawr stone circle.

Llyn y Fan Fawr.
(Photo: Nick Jenkins)

Llyn y Fan Fach.
(Photo: Nick Jenkins)

Llyn y Fan Fach.
(Photo: Nick Jenkins)

Remains of ancient tree trunk (circa 3000BC ?) exposed at low water at Llyn y Fan Fach.

Llyn y Fan Fach at low water.

Defensive perimeter walls of Y Garn Goch.

Castell Carreg Cennen.
(Photo: Nick Jenkins)

'Sarn Helen'. Note the Roman handiwork of the surface.

'Maen Madog' and 'Sarn Helen'.

Limestone pavements.

Castell Carreg Cennen.
(Photo: Nick Jenkins)

St Simon and St Judes Church, Llanddeusant.

This is the Parish Church of
Llanfihangel Talyllyn.
Llanfihangel Talyllyn. Church of St. Michael
At The head of the Lake.
The First Church on this site was built
between 700 & 1066. The Christian Church
Replaced a Pagan Temple.
The Tower & Nave are Ancient but not
the Windows. The Chancel was completely
rebuilt in 1870. The Font is Norman.
There are Four Bells. Two are dated 1678.
The Stone in the porch dates back to before the
Birth of Christ. Use unknown. It was placed
here on the eve of the disestablishment of
The Church in Wales in 1920.
This is none other than The House of God
& this is The Gate of heaven.

Stone Pillar in entrance porch of St Michael, Llanfihangel Talyllyn.

> •. This is the Parish Church of •.
> Llanfihangel Talyllyn.
> Llanfihangel Talyllyn. Church of St. Michael
> At The Head of the Lake.
> The First Church on this site was built
> between 700 & 1066. The Christian Church
> Replaced a Pagan Temple.
> The Tower & Nave are Ancient but not
> the Windows. The Chancel was completely
> rebuilt in 1870. The Font is Norman.
> There are Four Bells. Two are dated 1678.
> The Stone in the porch dates back to before the
> Birth of Christ. Use unknown. It was placed
> here on the eve of the disestablishment of
> . The Church in Wales in 1920. .
> This is none other than The house of God
> & this is The Gate of heaven.

Wording inside the porch at St Michael's Church, Talyllyn. (Llanfihangel Talyllyn).

St Michael's Church, Talyllyn. (Llanfihangel Talyllyn).

priority is to catch one's breath and familiarise with the surroundings. It is only when the pulse and breathing approaches normality and complaining muscles relax that the imagination is able to take flight. Many plausible and possible motives are offered about why these stones should have been erected. 'Of course . . . they are route markers!' exclaim some, but why seven when one would be sufficient? 'No, they are not route markers . . . they mark the site of some sacred ceremony! Or perhaps they are memorials to seven people?' say others, but no, that doesn't fit in with similar evidence from other sites of the period. 'Ah . . . but wait a minute . . . perhaps they are . . . ?' and so it goes on.

So here we have it. Saith Maen – seven ancient monoliths, some now recumbent and some upright, but all placed in alignment on an approximate north-north east setting on top of a lonely, windswept plateau. If I were to tell you that there is something else here, some other clue as to why these stones were set in this position, then I would be irresponsible. And yet –

Taking my compass, I take a bearing on the alignment, noting a heading of 18 to 20 degrees north-north west. This leads towards a deep and narrow valley some half a mile (800m) distant. Sighting along the opposite track, to the south, the line crosses the limestone scree and dips towards the southern extremity of the Swansea valley. If the alignment is a way marker then it begs the question – 'which way'? Standing here with the chill wind biting every unprotected area of pink flesh, it is tempting to follow the southern track. Nevertheless, knowing that there is little known prehistoric evidence in that direction, we decide to follow the northerly heading. Stepping in the venerable footprints of ancient ancestors, I button up my storm collar and bend into the wind. Hopefully we might be following the directions of a ghostly people whose ancient endeavours now transcend the thousands of years, leading us on a compass bearing towards who knows what?

Having walked a few hundred yards, we are soon brought to an abrupt halt by the incredible nature of the surroundings. A huge crater lies before us, and this is not the only one in the vicinity for this whole area is pock marked with depressions that are described on the Ordnance Map as *Shake holes* or *Swallow holes*. The geological term for such features is *Collapse Dolines*. The depressions are primarily caused by rainwater permeating down through the hard rock covering and dissolving the relatively softer limestone beneath. Eventually, without the underlying support of the limestone, the rock mantle collapses causing the subsequent depressions. In some cases, an alignment of several of these depressions will indicate the presence of an underground river or stream. Frequently, as here in Cwm Tawe, it all results in an impressive cave system such as 'Dan yr Ogof'. This area of the Brecon Beacons has the reputation of having the most extensive cave system in Europe, and the weird and wonderful landscape attracts cavers and potholers from all over the world to explore its subterranean wonders. You don't have to walk far on this mountain to see the innumerable holes, pits and openings that promise entry into the enchanting underworld. In a rocky cavern not far from here lies the sleeping *y Brenin Arthur* with his band of armour clad knights, waiting for the call to rise and once again take up arms to defend the homeland. It is here, somewhere beneath our feet, that *y Tylwyth Teg* roam the dark passages beneath Craig-y-nos, waiting for nightfall before they come out to wreak havoc in the streets of Ystradgynlais and beyond.

In his book *Folklore: Welsh & Manx* of 1901, Sir John Rhys wrote: 'The old folk used to say that there was a pit somewhere about the middle of the castle (Ynys Geinon rock) about a yard wide and some five or six yards deep with a stone about three tons in weight over the mouth of it, and they (the fairies) had a passage underground from the pit all the way to the cave at Dan yr Ogof, near the top of the Cwm, that is, near Adelina Patti's residence at Craig-y-nos Castle: there, it was said, they spent their time during the day, while they came down here (to Ystradgynlais) to play their tricks at night.'

More or less everyone believed in the existence of fairies during the early middle ages, and knew that one should never join in their fairy dance or enter a fairy ring without risking becoming enchanted. Geraldus Cambrensis relates in his journals that even educated people commonly accepted fairies, spirits and witchcraft. Many are the tales about the ancient powers and the nature spirits that inhabit these hills, and we can often catch a glimpse of an underlying truth in the legends and fables that have evolved from these tales during later periods in history. Although the stories seem to have no apparent relationship to what has gone before, they can sometimes hold a tenuous grasp on a bare thread of ancient truth and customs. Let us continue with the example already quoted, which is of particular interest to me and illustrates the point rather well.

In the ancient folklore of south Wales, retold in Sir John Rhys's account, there is a story that involves the mysterious disappearance of a farmer from the neighbourhood of Cwm Tawe. Briefly, it concerns the tale of a young man who discovered the password to a secret entrance into Ynys Geinon rock, near Craig-y-nos. The story goes on to tell about the youth finding a secret entrance to a network of caves and tunnels that ran in all directions, some leading to the caves at Dan yr Ogof, others to the caves at Ystradfellte and others to Garn Goch. The fairies he discovered living in these caves captured him and kept him with them for seven years, but he eventually escaped with a *hatful of guineas.*

Sir John Rhys tells of how the once captive man informed a farmer of the secret password. The farmer in turn went and found the entrance to this secret place: where he stole 'thrice the fill of a salt chest of guineas, half guineas, and seven and sixpenny pieces in one day. But he got too greedy; and like many a greedy one before him his crime proved his death; for he went down the fourth time in the dusk of the evening, when the fairies came upon him and he was never seen anymore.' The story goes on to say that, 'it is true enough that the above mentioned farmer got lost, and that nothing was heard respecting him'.

There seems to be no doubt that sometime in the distant past, a man living in the upper regions of Cwm Tawe disappeared in mysterious circumstances. Without any logical reason for his untimely disappearance, his capture by fairies became part of the local folklore. However, the story does not end there because, early in 1946, a group of men were to highlight this ancient folk tale and possibly provide conclusive evidence to explain its foundation.

Believing that a certain section of the mountainside known as Ogof Ffynnon Ddu concealed a vast cave complex, a group of individuals who were the forerunners of the 'South Wales Caving Club' discovered a subterranean system of caves in these hills, which they started to explore. Whilst researching this book I was overjoyed to speak to the sole survivor of that caving expedition, Mr Peter Harvey who, aged eighty, was still caving! He related the story of that day's events:

'We knew there was a cave there because we could hear the river running beneath our feet. There was no natural opening nearby so we had to dig down in the field. We dug down about fifteen feet (4.6m) and broke into the passageway. We knew we were in the right place because we could feel the draught rising in our faces, which is always a sure sign of a cave system. Some of our number went and explored a side passage and discovered some human remains! On hearing of this I, too, went into this side passage to see what they had found. We explored some distance before my cap lamp shone on something ahead of me, which I couldn't quite make out. I must admit I got a bit of a shock when my lamp lit up the remains of a human being; a skeleton in a crouched position on the floor in front of me. We couldn't understand how it came to be down there. There was a bit of a rock fall behind him, so he must have found his own way in through a shake hole. The entrance must have collapsed behind him, or maybe he was thrown down there.'

One can imagine the shock of coming upon some human remains inside a cave system that had until then no apparent opening to the outside world. Who was this person and how did he get in? How long had he been down there? The remains were subsequently removed and the whole episode subjected to much theory and speculation. Peter went on to explain that a fellow caver and archaeologist, Mr E Mason, spent a considerable time investigating the remains, but could not establish the age or epoch of this individual.

Armed with Peter Harvey's information, I set about trying to trace the skeleton and, on 27 March 2001, found myself in the Collections Department of The National Museums and Galleries Of Wales. I was staring at a cardboard box with the reference number 89.26H. In the bottom of this shallow and very humble little box lay the sad remains from Ogof Ffynnon Ddu. Under the glare of a powerful desk lamp I studied a yellowing fragment of femur. There were also two arm bones, most of one foot, and a number of teeth. Whilst there was no evidence to suggest the age or sex of the individual, it is thought that he was male and probably lived sometime from the Bronze Age to possibly the Roman period. Staring at the bones, my mind was filled with questions regarding the possibly awful events of his death. Had he fallen into this cavern because the weight of his footsteps finally broke through the already weakened and precarious rock mantle, ultimately half burying him in the process? Did he, like many later curious and eager cavers, decide to explore the depths of a shake hole, and become trapped as the roof collapsed behind him? Alternatively, was he the victim of some terrible event, with his remains being pushed down a convenient hole in the ground that was deliberately filled in behind him? Whatever the reason, could these be the remains of the 'greedy farmer' of the folktale?

This possible fulfilment of folklore illustrates spectacularly how legends may have an element of truth within the fantasy. It isn't hard to imagine the man's ultimate end, and neither is it difficult to imagine people trying to come to terms with his disappearance. With no clue as to what had occurred and no body, it was natural for superstitious people to assume that he had somehow wandered into the clutches of the fairies.

Mr Mason returned the rest of the remains to Ogof Ffynnon Ddu, a fitting and proper conclusion to this tale. Once again, these mountains will continue to encompass the life, the death, and the history of its ancient people, as represented by the age-old remains of my ancestors.

Grid Ref: SO 833155
Saith Maen

Taking the A4067, make for Craig-y-nos castle, which is situated on the Swansea side of the Dan yr Ogof show caves. From the castle entrance, cross the road and follow the designated footpath up Cribarth hill ahead of you. It is possible you may find that the designated footpaths have changed since this book was written, but whatever route you follow there is no way of avoiding a rather steep ascent to the top. The views however are well worth the effort.

Once you reach the top of Cribarth keep a sharp lookout for Saith Maen. It's advisable to follow map and compass as the path is not always well defined and it's easy to loose seven ancient stones amongst the rock and scree that litter this fascinating landscape.

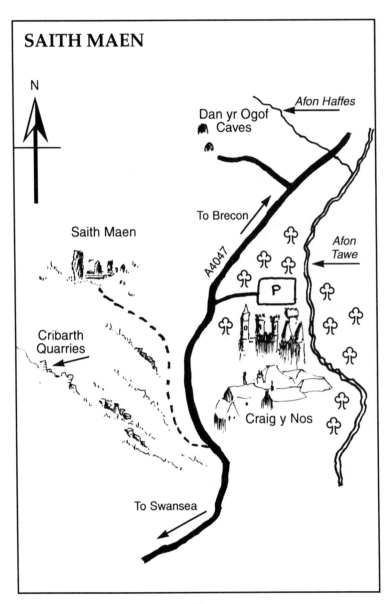

SAITH MAEN

N

Afon Haffes

Dan yr Ogof
Caves

To Brecon

A4047

Saith Maen

Afon Tawe

P

Cribarth
Quarries

Craig y Nos

To Swansea

Huts on Fan Hir
(An Impression)

Chapter Six

Hearth and Home

Walking in these hills, you can easily pass within a few feet of something wonderful and yet fail to recognise its significance. So it is with remnants of earlier habitations that quite often can be represented by little more than a jumble of rock, a tump of grass or by natural looking mounds that are not what they seem.

Once again following the heading set by Saith Maen, we cross Cwm Haffes and climb the opposite slope towards Fan Hir, heading for the *Hut circles* and *Field Systems* that are clearly marked on the Ordnance map. My fellow trekker Peter Daley points towards a feature on a distant rise and, moving forward, I struggle to make sense of what seems to be a vague and ill defined shape in the landscape. All that I can see is an indistinct line that runs at an angle across the hill, but he assures me that here are the remains of an ancient field system. Nearby he also indicates the rough outline of some primitive dwelling. A few yards further and we come across an insignificant kidney shaped lump that is marked on our Ordnance map as *Burnt Mound*. Earthen mounds such as this can easily be mistaken for natural features and passed without a second glance. There is some debate as to their original purpose, but as they are usually found near a source of water and contain a high content of burnt material within their structure, they are thought to mark a primitive cooking site.

Standing here amidst the ancient hut circles and field systems, one can imagine the life and circumstances of the people that lived in this mountain settlement. There is a pattern here that gives rise to images that can be constructed from what has been deduced from evidence obtained at Waun Fignen Felen and elsewhere. It is known that, over time, the rough boulder and hawthorn dominated landscape gradually evolved into one of wooded slopes by the Neolithic Age (circa 3000BC), with the vegetation thinning slightly on the hills. It is also known that people had developed from the hunter/gatherers of the Mesolithic Age into farmers who lived in settled communities, and had somewhat developed their technology in the intervening period. Hunting for food however was still a central part of their existence.

The cooking site itself is of much interest and, although it is pure conjecture as to how exactly the food would actually be cooked, evidence collected from a number of similar sites that have been identified has caused some interesting theories. It is thought, since the mounds almost invariably occur near a shallow source of water, that stones and rocks were placed in the fire and then moved into the water so as to heat it. However, the likelihood of heating the water sufficiently to boil a joint of venison or wild boar seems rather farfetched, and an interesting alternative suggestion is that the stones were heated so as to create an early form of sauna or 'sweat box'. This seems to be supported by similar findings amongst the Native American population.

Crossing Fan Hir is by normal standards quite simple, in fact little more than an afternoon's stroll. One has to always however be aware on these high, open and unsheltered mountains of what's going on. Even when fully equipped, the body is still vulnerable should these mountains undergo a serious mood change. The late seasonal snow patches that appear to lie on level ground can in truth conceal a vicious shake hole that will snap your leg at the shin or knee joint as you step into it. But the weather, which often changes so suddenly, can be the most awesome and fearful element of all.

Peter's surprised gasp makes me turn abruptly. Following his pointed finger I catch sight of the ominous black clouds that have suddenly materialised from nowhere and I watch in trepidation as the sky begins to darken. Within minutes the first snowflakes begin to tumble, fluttering down like innocent confetti but at the same time heralding possible disaster. Certainly, the few remnants of January snowfall still lie where the spring sunshine has not yet touched, but this is May! We started under a clear blue sky but the wind has suddenly changed direction and, at this altitude, the effects are dramatic. I fasten the storm collar of my jacket and lift the hood. Raising my eyes to the distant northern summit of Fan Brycheiniog, I watch in fascination as the peak seems to claw at the mass of tumbling clouds that are now streaming and flaring across the heights. We both realise that we have to get off this mountain fairly quickly.

Before us, the air is filled with a scurrying, scrambling mass of snowflakes. Typically, neither is willing to admit our concern at this stage since we know that somewhere in front of us is a small track to safety. The problem is that the track leads down a very steep rock escarpment. I stop and check the map; the compass confirms that our heading takes us towards what the tightly grouped contour lines indicate to be a steep and possibly dangerous descent. With the snow now covering every reasonable feature and the ground beginning to drop away, I hope that the transition from horizontal to sheer vertical is a gradual affair. We know that we have to get close to the edge before we can catch sight of the route downwards. In normal conditions, this is a simple matter but, with visibility deteriorating, we have to reconsider our plans. We stand and mull over all the options when suddenly my eyes fall upon a small unnatural feature.

About half a metre in front of us, a small cairn of stones are rapidly turning into a pile of snowballs, and would have become just another snow covered mound if we hadn't arrived when we did. I punch the air in triumph, say a prayer of thanks and yell out my gratitude to every like-minded and similarly suffering hill walker who has passed this way. Pausing to wipe the snowflakes from my glasses, I turn to my companion and point to the man made pile of stones that marks the track down to safety. Suddenly, the experiential truth of some of the standing stones on our hills and mountains has become a little clearer.

Almost certainly, the larger more dramatic monoliths on our mountains have an inherently powerful spiritual connection. However some, including perhaps Saith Maen, could be simple route markers. Having experienced at first hand the dangerous changes in weather conditions in these mountains, these isolated stones are definitely very effective way markers or signposts. Anyone who doubts the validity of this argument should visit the pitiful memorial stone to little Tommy Jones in the foothills of Pen y Fan. The story of this tragic incident is for another time and another place, but it should be compulsive telling for all that seek to explore these hills because it reinforces their inherent danger in a disturbing manner.

The descent of the east face is uncomfortable, with the light snow making progress down the steep narrow track an anxious experience. Eventually we reached the lower slopes and the ominous grey clouds soon begin to dissipate. At this lower altitude, the snow is falling as light rain. The sun begins to shine through the dissolving clouds as we head down with renewed optimism, and a new spring in our step.

Grid Ref: SN 837177
Hearth and Home

From the ancient river bed of Cwm Haffes, strike out upwards to ascend the lower slopes of Fan Hir, where evidence of early settlement have been found in the form of hut circles, field systems and burnt mounds.

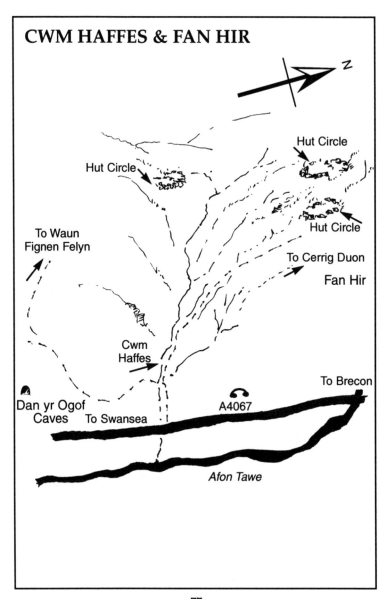

CWM HAFFES & FAN HIR

N

Hut Circle

Hut Circle

Hut Circle

To Waun
Fignen Felyn

To Cerrig Duon

Fan Hir

Cwm
Haffes

To Brecon

Dan yr Ogof
Caves   To Swansea   A4067

Afon Tawe

Cerrig Duon and Maen Mawr

Chapter Seven

Cerrig Duon

Descending the narrow track from the mountain, I cannot help pre-empting the first glimpse of the new mystery that awaits us. My anticipation of viewing this remarkable sight at close quarters is obvious as we make our way down from the snow line, and the earlier tiredness and anxiety disappears as we reach level ground. Crossing several fast flowing mountain streams, we trek our purposeful way across the barren foothills, maintaining as far as possible the heading indicated by Saith Maen.

Like any journey of discovery, the closer one gets, the longer it takes. This was certainly true of this mini expedition. Each hillock, each rise in the ground tantalises us with the promise of a view from its opposite side, but disappointingly fails to deliver. My legs begin to take on a motion of their own as the unnatural effort of walking across the sideways sloping ground puts uneven demands on back and hips. Suddenly however, we round a small headland, and for the first time see the remote, lonely and haunting presence of *Cerrig Duon*.

Seeing it here from the high foothills of Fan Fechan is to be swamped by sensations that seem to touch at ancient, long forgotten memories. To come to Cerrig Duon after a long and arduous journey is an experience that is both exciting, and awesome. As we draw closer, I am filled with vague, yet strangely pleasurable sensations of relief, joy and welcome, which at the time I don't understand, but on later reflection see within the context of this megalithic monument. The last half-mile seems never ending, but we forget our weariness and increase our pace in eager impatience.

To come here via the hills is to experience history with new emphasis, for this is a place that thrusts ancient realities and echoes upon you in a rush of sensations. We immediately dropped our rucksacks to stand in awed silence at this enigma; struggling and striving to make sense of it.

Cerrig Duon is a circular formation of individual stones of approximately 30cm to 45cm in height. The perimeter is approximately 58.2m and, situated on its northernmost curve is a medium sized standing stone known as *Maen Mawr*, which is some 2m in height. The whole complex is aligned on a north-south axis, and sits on a natural plateau. A few metres to the east, the infant Afon Tawe tumbles from the foothills. Compared to other more notable sites, Cerrig Duon with its stunted formation of individual stones must come very low in the list of desirable megalithic monuments. Indeed, it appears that several of the original stones have been removed, the site having suffered from despoliation. Even during the three-year period that I have been visiting the place, some have been removed and replaced by smaller, inferior substitutes. However, to judge Cerrig Duon in terms of size, status, and structure is to miss the real significance of this remarkable place, for there is one attribute that singles out this monument from some of the more illustrious specimens. This site is one of only ten in the UK with an oval layout of stones rather than the more typical circle. Similarly, it has an untypical three stone setting in that Maen Mawr is the larger of a set of three, the other two being very small outliers directly to the rear. In addition, a short distance to the east is an avenue, some 42m in length, of small stones running up to the plateau from the same heading.

Like the tomb builders, the people who built Cerrig Duon were concerned with ritual and continuity. This ritualistic principle spans the ages like a thread through a tapestry, touching every age and generation. Cerrig Duon is no exception, and was a focus point for Bronze Age people who populated these hills sometime during the 2nd millennium BC.

Taking the time to ponder on how this place must have

looked before these stones were laid I am reminded of the ancient peat bog of Waun Fignen Felen, some 100 metres higher in altitude, and approximately 2 kilometres to the west of this spot. Archaeological excavations and vegetational analysis at Waun Fignen Felen identified pollen samples of Birch, Hazel, and Elm, present at various stages throughout thousands of years of prehistory. In the knowledge of those findings I am aware that the plateau on which I now stand, being considerably lower in elevation than the peat bog, must have once been covered in trees; the climate being considerably warmer and the soil much richer. Here in the valley, with the heights above providing shelter from the chill breeze, the early spring sunshine would be warm and fresh. It is easy to imagine how the trees on the plateau would provide a natural woodland glade. Tired from our exertions, Peter and I sit on our rucksacks and discuss the likely motives of the people who created this special place. Soon our combined fantasies create a scenario that moves from the possible into the probable: and so begins the second part of our journey, which is of the imagination.

The broad-leafed oaks provide a natural canopy diffusing the spring sunlight in dancing, shifting shades of green. Somewhere in the distant undergrowth, a wild boar squeals its alarm and scurries away towards the security of the densely wooded valley floor. Gradually the hills around begin to ring with the sound of distant voices that rise and fall in a medley of excited laughter and song. Individual family groups that include men, women, young children and elders are walking down from the peaks, their voices raised in excited chatter. On the fringes of this excited column, young men armed with flint tipped spears keep a constant watch of the higher ground whilst mangy hunting dogs bound in expectant anticipation before them, their eager eyes never diverting from the faces of their masters. A further cacophony of sound descend from the hills to the left as a second, larger column of people appears over the lower slopes. As the two opposing columns come into view the hills erupt in a symphony of excited gesticulation and song. Soon, arms and spears are raised and waved across the valley to the accompaniment of shrill warbling cries, as both groups congregate on this special spot.

Soon the area around the black stone of Maen Mawr, which was placed here by their ancestors, is filled with excited, chattering groups. An elder steps forward from between the oaks, arms raised, and shouts a command. Immediately, bronze axes are laid to the small saplings sprouting from the centre of the plateau, and within a short period, a clearing develops extending to the wooded perimeter. When the task is completed, the men select rocks from the many that litter these hills. As the day moves on, holes are dug in the soil in preparation to receive the stones.

In response to something operating at a deep level, these ancient people chose this mountain glade around Maen Mawr as the page on which to write their deepest, heartfelt statement. In this reflective moment, I shared their relief at the completion of a long and perhaps dangerous journey to this scared place, and the joy and welcome of once again bonding with old friends and family in community and unity of purpose.

What is it about this remote plateau that attracted so many of our ancestors? Why the long trek from distant homesteads down into deeply wooded valleys, which always posed a threat to these deeply superstitious people. However much the established religions of today seek to distance themselves from such pagan sites, the fact remains that the power that motivated these people was the stirring of an infant spirituality. The fact that it was sometimes expressed in strange and disturbing ways does not deny its origins. The fault lies not in the inspiration but in its interpretation. The worship of the natural world in all its beauty and awe-inspiring order, whilst primitive and misplaced, does not negate the source of the inspiration or the power that drove it. To deny the spirit that drove these primitive people in their ignorance is to deny the creator himself, and a blasphemy equal to anything our ancestors could have conceived in their primitive, yet innocent struggle towards truth.

Before the season is out, ritual praise, prayer and memorial will be celebrated here. Long after the end of the age, this site will be venerated by others who will tell their children, and their children's children, of the ancient people who created it. This is a place that will always be held sacred long after the reason for its foundation has been forgotten. It is a place that would come to be visited and used much later by a new generation of truth seekers. This is the continuity that will span the ages and the generations, manifesting itself in the many and varied ways that we choose to reach out to our gods. Cerrig Duon was one of these ways, and it was another step towards the infinite reality.

'I have seen for myself how extremely scrupulous you are in all religious matters, because I noticed, as I strolled round admiring your sacred monuments, that you had an alter inscribed: To an unknown God. **Well, the God whom I proclaim is in fact the one whom you already worship without knowing it.** Acts Ch 17: V 22: 23

Grid Ref: SN 852206
Cerrig Duon

Take the A4067 Swansea to Brecon Road until you come to Tafarn-y-Garreg, a public house situated about three quarters of a mile (1km) on the Brecon side of the Dan yr Ogof caves.

Almost opposite the pub, on the Brecon side, an unclassified road leads to the village of Trecastell/Trecastle, several miles distant. Follow this road until it starts to run parallel with a small river, on your left. At this point keep your eyes on the slopes on the far side of the river as the only indication you will have of the site will be the large standing stone that forms part of the Cerrig Duon stone circle. This stone is Maen Mawr, and indicates the northern edge of the site. There are a few small pull ins, where you can park your car, before crossing the stream to reach Cerrig Duon.

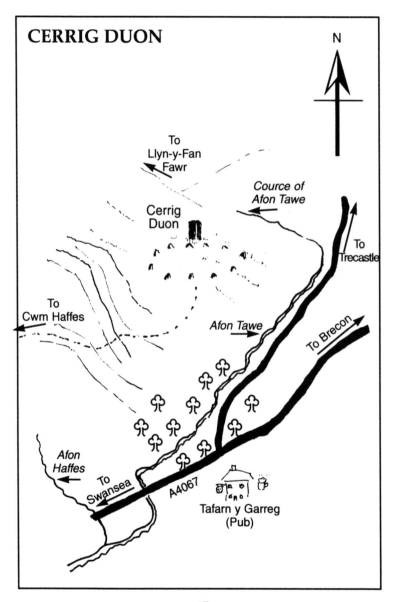

CERRIG DUON

N

To
Llyn-y-Fan
Fawr

Cource of
Afon Tawe

Cerrig
Duon

To
Trecastle

To
Cwm Haffes

Afon Tawe

To Brecon

Afon
Haffes

To
Swansea

A4067

Tafarn y Garreg
(Pub)

Llyn y Fan Fawr

Chapter Eight

Lakes and Legends
'Llyn y Fan Fawr'

No visit to Cerrig Duon is complete without undertaking a pilgrimage to another primitive location that has long stirred the imagination. Indeed, it could be said with justification that people have been visiting Llynnoedd y Fan for eight to ten thousand years!

Beneath the towering rock escarpments that make up this area of mountain known as Y Bannau lie two very enigmatic and famous lakes. It is easy to unwind in the timelessness of these hills, gradually letting the world get on with itself whilst you become lost in the hypnotic hiss and gurgle of tiny, crystal waterfalls. It is here, at approximately 550 metres in elevation, that the foothills of Fan Brycheiniog give birth to a stream that is driven by an urgent need to become Afon Tawe.

The highest point on this majestic ridge of old red sandstone is Fan Brycheiniog, having a spot height of 802 metres. This is the second highest peak in Bannau Brycheiniog *(the Brecon Beacons)*. Its sister summit, and next-door neighbour, is Fan Foel at 781 metres. The climb to the base of the summit is not hazardous provided you follow the well-worn tracks of previous visitors. Whilst the maps give an indication of the pathways, it's advisable to use a little common sense and keep an eye on the vegetation that can signal a patch of marshy ground. Distances can be deceiving, and whilst the trek is not too severe, the mountain can appear to be closer; forever seeming to be just over the next ridge! Soon you approach the mighty east facing rock wall of Fan Hir, and nestling at the base of this amphitheatre like escarpment you will find the enchanting and beguiling waters of Llyn y Fan Fawr. If this sounds a little romantic then so be it, for romance itself was defined in these hills. But beware, because up here enchantment lies in wait for the unwary in all its bewitching power. This is where the unknown and unseen come alive!

For hundreds of years, the people of Brecon until fairly recently made an annual pilgrimage to these lakes to witness an annual event that was said to have taken place on the First Sunday of August. In his *Celtic Folklore: Welsh & Manx*, John Rhys recalls a conversation with a Bishop of Asaph.

'An old woman from Myddfai who is now, that is to say in January 1881, about eighty years of age, tells me that she remembers "thousands and thousands of people visiting the Lake of the Little Fan on the first Sunday or Monday in August, and when she was young she often heard old men declare that at that time a commotion took place in the lake, and that its waters boiled, which was taken to herald the approach of the Lake Lady and her Oxen"

John Rhys continued by relating a second version of this folktale, given in an account of a conversation he had with a Mr Davies, schoolteacher of Ystalyfera.

'It has been the yearly custom (for generations as far as I can find) for young as well as many people further advanced in years to make a general excursion in carts, gambos and all kinds of vehicles, to Llyn y Fan, in order to see the water nymph (who appeared on one day only, viz. the first Sunday in August.) This nymph was said to have the lower part of her body resembling that of a dolphin, while the upper part was that of a beautiful lady (if the lake should be without a ripple) and combed her tresses on the reflecting surface of the lake. The yearly peregrination to the abode of the Fan deity is still kept up in this valley – Cwm Tawe; but not to the extent that it used to formerly.'

Skirting the edge of this lake, you have to stop and pay respect, because this mountain has held power over the people who lived beneath its towering heights since they first set foot on its slopes. The water that springs from these hills and forms this lake is the source of dreams and folklore. Visit it and discover for yourself that this is indeed a land of fairies, nymphs and heroes. In the clear sunshine of autumn, the summit is mirrored in the water, the image occasionally being disturbed by a light breeze from the peaks. The silence of the place is overwhelming, for it is only disturbed by the occasional whisper of the wind.

As the fabric of a church retains echoes of sanctity, this place holds powerful emotions from the near and ancient past. Sitting at the water's edge the stillness envelops you. Soon you cannot fail to sense a procession of countless hundreds who have made the journey to this most serenely beautiful place, each leaving a little of themselves behind whilst imbuing the mountain with a magic and mystery that transcends time and dimension. But this is no ordinary mountain and this is no ordinary lake. Here is where an ancient people first raised their eyes to the peaks and their minds to the unknown in an undefinable need to know. This is as sacred as a mountain gets.

Grid Ref: SN 830215

Lakes and Legends
'Llyn y Fan Fawr'

Following the unclassified road to Trecastell, we leave Cerrig Duon and climb a little higher until Afon Tawe starts to distance itself from the road. At this point we leave the road and follow the young river upward through the foothills heading for the base of the mighty rock face above us. Keeping this impressive escarpment ever before us, we eventually reach Llyn y Fan Fawr. Be careful of the marshy ground.

LLYN Y FAN FAWR

LLYN Y FAN FAWR

Z

Course of Afon Tawe

To Trecastle

Cerrig
Duon

Standing
Stone

To A4067

Llyn y Fan Fach

Chapter Nine

Dark Depths
'Llyn y Fan Fach'

It is but a relatively short trek from Llyn y Fan Fawr to another ancient and fabled location. Following a track northwest around the base of the Fannau, you come upon a second lake – Llyn y Fan Fach. Similar in situation and altitude, it is as different in character as it is in spirit. The enchanting romance that is Llyn y Fan Fawr has been left on the other side of the mountain. You are now on the dark side!

If ever a location deserves a legend, then Llyn y Fan Fach certainly does. If there were none, this dark and brooding expanse of water would conjure up its own. This could easily lay claim to where mighty 'Caledfwlch' *(Excalibur)* was first raised aloft from the deep. This is the place where ravens swoop from the summits of the Fannau, their death rattle croaks echoing the black hearted triumphant cry of wicked Morgan Le Fay: this 'dark, passionate, handsome woman; so proficient in the dark and destructive magic' as John Steinbeck described her in his *The Acts of King Arthur and his Noble Knights*. Standing here at the lake edge with a circling buzzard riding the thermal air above me, I would subscribe to any ancient tale. In fact, Llyn y Fan Fach is the subject of one of the most renowned Welsh legends of all, and one which must be recollected at each and every visit to this spectacular place – *The Legend Of The Lady Of The Lake*.

'When the eventful struggle made by the Princes of South Wales to preserve the independence of their country was drawing to a close in the twelfth century, there lived at Blaensawde near Llanddeusant, Carmarthenshire, a widowed woman, the relict of a farmer who had fallen on disastrous troubles.'

The tale goes on to explain that this unfortunate widow had a son who, one day, was watching over the cattle up near Llyn y Fan Fach when to his astonishment he saw a beautiful lady sitting on the water combing her hair. Completely bewitched, he offered her some bread and cheese, which was his meal for the day. The beautiful woman refused, saying; 'Cras dy fara. Nid hawdd fy nala' (*Hard baked is thy bread. Tis not easy to catch me*), whereupon she quickly disappeared beneath the dark waters. Later, telling his mother what he had seen, she advised him that next time he should take some unbaked dough with him.

He returned to the lake several times and on the third visit the lady reappeared. This time she accepted his offer of the bread, and consented to be his wife. She would bring with her as a dowery a herd of wonderful cattle. However, she told him that if he ever struck her three blows without cause, she would leave him forever – 'tair ergyd ddiachos' (*three causeless blows*). He agreed never to do such a thing and the happy couple went to live at a farm near the village of Myddfai, becoming parents of three sons who were said to have been very beautiful children.

One day, the couple were invited to a christening. On the morning of the event, the young woman was reluctant to go. In an effort to hurry her along, her husband slapped her shoulder with his glove, saying, 'dos, dos!' (*go, go!*) She then reminded him of the agreement and warned him to be more careful in future. On a later occasion when they were at a wedding, his wife suddenly started to cry. Embarrassed by her behaviour he tapped her on the shoulder, asking why she was behaving in this fashion. She replied, 'Now people are entering into trouble, and your troubles are likely to commence, as you have the second time stricken me without a cause'.

Many years later, the children had grown up and had

Mesolithic Pieces

Greensand Cwert Fragment
L:23.9 W:18.3 Th:3.8
Waun Fignen Felyn

Pale Grey Flint Piece
L:36.1 W:9.8 Th:4.0
Llyn y Fan Fach

**Pale Grey with Possible
Retouch**
L:31.6 W:16.3 Th:3.7
Llyn y Fan Fach

Dark Grey Piece
L:26.8 W:20.4 Th:5.5
Llyn y Fan Fach

become very clever men. His wife often reminded him to be careful that he would not give the third and final blow, which through circumstances beyond her control would separate them eternally. One day, they were together at a funeral when suddenly his wife began to laugh. Alarmed, her husband touched her, saying, 'Hush! Hush! Don't laugh!' She replied 'I laugh because people, when they die, go out of trouble.' Rising up, she went out, saying 'the last blow has been struck, our marriage contract is broken and at an end; farewell.' She then returned to the farm where she called together all her cattle, and made her way back to Llyn y Fan Fach. On returning to the lake, she walked into the water, disappearing beneath the surface with the cattle following closely behind!

Normally, legends and folklore would end there, but this one is unique as it continues by illustrating how the three sons of the Lady of the Lake, far from accepting the loss of their mother, returned frequently to Llyn y Fan Fach in order to search for her. They were not disappointed, because on one occasion the mother appeared to her eldest son, Rhiwallon, and told him that his lifetime mission would be to relieve people of pain and misery through healing. To help in his work she gave him a bag containing many treatments for the preservation of health. Tradition and history records that the three sons did in fact become physicians, and were known collectively as 'Meddygon Myddfai' *(the Physicians of Myddfai)*.

There are several different versions of this story. Some refer to the lady being struck by iron; some say all the cattle were white, whilst other versions tell the tale differently. In his excellent *A History of Wales*, John Davies writes of the significant changes brought about by the Iron Age (circa 500BC). 'Those knowing the secret of iron-making represented a threat to those ignorant of the secret.' Mr Davies goes on to explain that there is an echo of that threat in the story of The Lady of the Lake; she being a symbol of the old order represented by her magic and her white cattle, returning to her world on being struck three

Later Neolithic / Bronze Age

Flake Fragment
L:26.2 W:20.04 Th:4.4
Llyn y Fan Fach

Flake Blade
L:46.2 W:28.5 Th:5.8
Llyn y Fan Fach

Flake Black Flint
L:24.6 W:28.5 Th:5.8
Llyn y Fan Fach

Carboniferous Cwert Flake
L:23.1 W:27.4 Th:7.0
Waun Fignen Felyn

times with iron. I based my rendering of the story on the more complete folktale as described in *Celtic Folklore: Welsh & Manx.* Sir John acknowledges his source for this folktale as being the version by Mr Rees of Tonn in his *The Physicians of Myddfai,* published by the Welsh Manuscript Society in 1861. Mr Rees claims his source to be from oral recitations by the residents of the village of Myddfai.

In similar lakes throughout Wales, there is evidence of sacrificial objects being cast into the waters in the form of tools, weapons, ornamental items, jewellery and other artefacts. In 1911, the lake at Llyn Fawr, Hirwaun in Mid Glamorgan, which lies just outside the southern boundary of The Brecon Beacons National Park, was drained in order to construct a reservoir. In the peat bottom were found bronze axe heads, chisels, a bronze clasp and belt fitting, some breast ornaments, a cauldron and other implements, this being a typically Celtic practice of the time. Similarly, in 1943 a hoard of bronze and iron objects, including spears, swords, shields, iron rims for chariot wheels, bridle bits, cauldrons and, more disturbingly, an iron 'gang chain' complete with neck shackles were recovered from the depths of Llyn Cerrig Bach on Ynys Môn *(Anglesey).* Were these iron 'neck' shackles cast into the waters as an offering in their own right, or dare we contemplate a more disturbing possibility?

Despite the sometimes oppressive and brooding nature of Llyn y Fan Fach, nothing had ever been found to suggest that this landscape had captured the imagination of our ancestors, spiritually or otherwise. There was never any archaeological evidence to support the notion that any of our prehistoric ancestors ever visited the area of this lake. I had always found this strange, and have never been able to accept that they would not visit this place; a fact that seemed to destroy the theory of continuity of purpose and attraction. With this denunciation ringing in our heads, Peter and I decided to make a combined effort and search the ground near the base of the eroded peat shoreline.

Starting at the eastern edge we progressed in a clockwise direction, scanning the waters edge, which thankfully seemed to have receded following a dry spell. I was amazed to see ancient tree trunks of oak and silver birch clamped and preserved within the black peat banks that surrounded the lake. Knowing that no trees had grown here for thousands of years instantly brought the past to life as I realised that I was now looking back in time! Prodding one of these ancient tree trunks, I was amazed to see that the distinctive bark of the silver birch seemed as fresh now as the day it was first enveloped by its peat black shroud!

Skirting the remainder of the shoreline we eventually reached the northern edge, and after a lengthy search, began to accept that the finds at Waun Fignen Felen must have been unique, when suddenly my eye caught a minute, whitish stone fragment. Picking it up I could see it was a crudely fashioned flint blade, or microlith as it is more accurately described. Strangely, in that moment, an inexplicable sense of timelessness swept over me. Despite the centuries that had passed, I felt that I was intruding upon someone else's property. I felt uncomfortable, its ancient owner suddenly standing close beside me. In my excitement I longed to shout out, but at the same time I wanted to hold on to the moment, alone with my thoughts and feelings. Soon, the thrill of the find was enveloped in sensations of awe and wonder at the significance of what I now held in the palm of my hand.

It is very difficult to try to describe such moments as these. To be the first to hold this item since it was dropped, or discarded, some six to eight thousand years ago is an experience that I am unable to share. The very act of picking it up from the earth seems to transport you back to the time and the circumstances of its loss. Indeed, studying its design and workmanship, you can almost sense the spirit of the man who fashioned, and later used it. At a purely subjective level, I found it a humbling experience. I was the first person to touch this object for possibly ten thousand years: it is awe inspiring to realise the time scale involved.

Thrilled by our success we resumed our search with renewed vigour until we had found several other flint artefacts and rough flint debris lying some five to six feet from the eroded peat shoreline, giving evidence of 'flint knapping,' having taken place at this site. Excited, yet unsure of the authenticity of what we had found, we tempered our exuberance until we could confirm our finds.

Some weeks later the staff at The National Museum of Wales, Cardiff, examined the finds and confirmed their authenticity, suggesting that possibly three of the flints were of the Mesolithic period, whilst two other blades were of Neolithic or Bronze Age. This in itself was a time span of approximately five to six thousand years!

Obviously, Llyn y Fan Fach was, and still is, a place that has attracted men and women. The lake has provided them with a valuable source of food, and the preserved tree trunks embedded within the peat provide ample evidence to show that this lake was, like Waun Fignen Felen, bordered by trees and other vegetation. Like Waun Fignen Felen, the hunters would have been able to use the cover provided by the woodland to stalk their prey to within a few metres, and the finding of these flint objects once again shows how this lake was once a generous provider for the prehistoric families that roamed these peaks. Whether or not it was a focus of religious ceremony or sacrifice remains to be discovered. Llyn-y Fan Fach, whilst beautiful and bewitching can also be a sinister, overpowering presence of a place. A lake of dark water where long forgotten fears and black deeds rise to the surface. It is the kind of place where primitive notions of earth, fire and water may have been acknowledged and celebrated.

I am aware that the legend of The Lady of the Lake has its origins in the twelfth century, but I believe that the roots of the story go far deeper. The fact that the lady seemed to be under some sort of spell, or committed to the inevitable, is disturbing. Could not this story, like the young farmer and the fairy treasure, be a long remembered but half-forgotten folk memory. The story would probably be distorted, developed and possibly reconstituted over time in a more palatable form? Whatever the truth, I feel that submerged beneath the dark, north facing chill waters of Llyn y Fan Fach lies the awful truths of some of the more primitive practices that our ancestors undertook in their desperate, yet misguided desire to know and appease their gods. Whilst there is no evidence, I would suggest that should the lake ever be drained and the bottom excavated, then that the dark and forbidding waters of Llyn y Fan Fach will give up its secrets.

Grid Ref: SN 800217

Dark Depths
'Llyn y Fan Fach'

There are two routes to Llyn y Fan Fach. If you have walked to its sister lake, Llyn y Fan Fawr, you can continue around the base of the two peaks until you reach the smaller lake. However, if travelling by car, there is an alternative route:

Take the A4069 that runs between Llangadog and Brynaman. Eventually you will enter a beautifully wooded valley some 4 kms from Llangadog, where you will reach an unclassified road crossing Afon Sawdde at Pontarllechau. Follow this road to Llanddeusant.

At Llanddeusant you will reach the parish church of St Simon and St Jude. Continue on past the church, heading for Llyn y Fan Fach which is signposted. Eventually the road will convert to a rough trackway alongside the river. Park your vehicle near here and walk up to the lake that sits below the distant Bannau Sir Gaer.

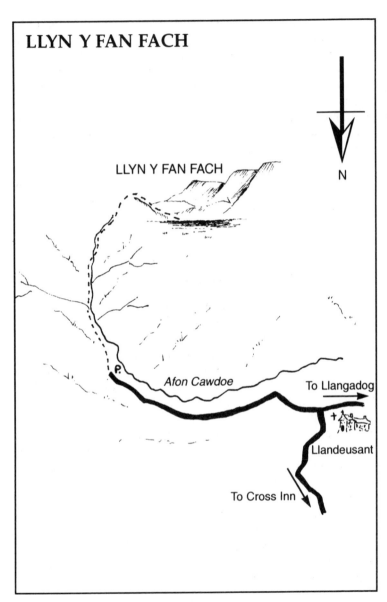

LLYN Y FAN FACH

LLYN Y FAN FACH

N

Afon Cawdoe

To Llangadog

Llandeusant

To Cross Inn

Maen Madog and Sarn Helen

Chapter Ten

Sarn Helen

Let us now return to the hills above the ancient riverbed of Cwm Pwll-y-rhyd in order to visit another impressive feature. Heading upstream from the ancient valley, we cross the river to ascend the upper reaches of Fan Nedd, one of several mountains that make up the central sector of the Brecon Beacons National Park. After fording the river, we reach the opposite bank and continue our ascent towards the crest. Soon the rough stone surface of the track begins to dissipate, and suddenly we are walking a wonder!

Beneath your feet lie an exposed section of stone slabs, which unlike the naturally occurring rock outcrops, are set into the mountain in ordered alignment. The transition from rough track to a regular, structured surface is gradual; nonetheless, the contrast is astounding! You soon realise that this is no hastily constructed track built by some busy farmer or forester. No, this is the work of a technological and culturally advanced master race who first entered these islands almost two thousand years ago, leaving a legacy of roads still to be found bisecting the mountains and hills. These stone highways were the work of the Romans.

This surface was laid down to ease the passage of an army of occupation, which had swept westward up the Thames valley towards the Severn from Kent and the low counties, and were now concentrating their Legion between two camps at Roman Neath and Brecon. However, you can always trust the Welsh to add a little colour to the dusty pages of history.

The origins of this road and the motives for building it are well known to the people of this land and have nothing to do with what Rome, or anyone else wanted. Indeed, if you want a little colour then you need look no further than Welsh legend.

In the history of Wales, one ancient book amongst many stands far above others in its pedigree. *Y Mabinogion* is a collection of eleven medieval Welsh stories recorded between the second half of the eleventh century and the end of the thirteenth, but composed far earlier. Most of these anonymous tales are concerned with Welsh mythology and folklore, and are preserved in two manuscripts: *The White Book of Rhydderch*, (c1300-1325) and the *Red Book of Hergest*, (c1375-1425). Lady Charlotte Guest who translated these stories in 1838 gave the title *Mabinogion* to the four fables that begin the collection but not to the remainder, one of which is entitled: *The Dream Of Macsen Wledig*.

In this tale, Macsen Wledig, emperor of Rome, had a dream whereby he sailed to 'the fairest island in the whole world'. In the island he saw a great castle, 'the roof of the great hall seemed to be all gold; the walls of the hall seemed to be entirely of glittering precious gems'. In his dream Macsen came upon the most beautiful woman he had ever seen, and was so smitten by her that when he awoke from his dream his whole spirit was pervaded by the memory of the beautiful maiden. The wise men of Rome were eventually brought to him, and he said to them: 'Sages of Rome, I have seen a dream, and in this dream I beheld a maiden, and because of the maiden is there neither life, nor spirit, nor existence within me.' 'Lord,' they answered, 'since thou judgest us worthy to counsel thee, we will give thee counsel. And this is our counsel; that thou should send messengers for three years to the three parts of the world, to seek for thy dream. And thou knowest not what day or what night good news may come to thee, the hope thereof will support thee.'

Eventually the messengers returned and following this Macsen journeyed to Eryri *(Snowdonia)* in the Island of Britain, where he found the maiden of his dreams, one *Elen Luyddog*. On seeing her seated on a chair of gold, he called out to her, '*Empress of Rome, all hail'!* and threw his arms about her neck, and that night she became his bride. It was agreed part of her dowry would be the construction of three castles: one at *Arfon,* one at *Caerllion,* and one at *Caerfyrddin.* Later Helen instigated the construction of roads between her castles.

'Then Helen bethought her to make high roads from one castle to another throughout the island of Britain. And the roads were made. And for this cause they are called the roads of <u>Helen</u> Luyddawc, that she was sprung from a native of this island, and the men of the island of Britain would not have made these great roads for any save her.' This account is taken from the translation of the Mabinogion by Charlotte Guest.

Now anyone with a little sense will tell you that this story is a piece of romantic nonsense. Whatever the truth, there are some interesting parallels to this tale which should be considered. A Roman General in the Island of Britain during the Roman occupation was a Magnus Maximus. This was the man the Welsh knew as Macsen Wledig. In 383 he declared himself Roman Emperor and gained control of Gaul and Spain before he was defeated by the Eastern emperor Theodorus I. It has been suggested that his removal of troops from Wales to aid his campaign led to the eventual collapse of Roman power in Britain. The medieval Welsh looked upon Macsen Wledig with particular high regard because of his marriage to a Welsh princess, Elen or the 'Helen Luyddog' of the Dream of Macsen Wledig. In fact this particular road, high up in the central sector of the National Park is known as Sarn Helen, *(Helens road).* It is claimed that the construction of this, and other Roman roads in Wales were at the instigation of this remarkable woman, and named so in memory of her prominent role as the wife of the Roman Emperor Magnus Maximus.

At the time that this surface was laid, the Romans had undoubtedly occupied the country for several hundred years and seen their culture and sophisticated system of administration become an accepted model for a new civil order. It was only a matter of time before a great many of the native people would regard themselves as *Romano Brython*, both in lineage and culture. However, these new ideas and social structures were not the only concepts to become absorbed by the population at large. Following on the heels of the military conquest came a new religion that challenged the pagan theology of the old Celtic peoples.

Persecution of the Christian church ended when Constantine the Great issued the Edict of Milan in 313, which mandated toleration of Christians within the Roman Empire. Later, Constantine himself was to be fully converted to the faith, and was baptised a Christian shortly before his death in 337.

Despite their successful and total control of the lowland zones, the Roman military were constantly aware of the possibility of attack from our early Welsh ancestors. However, despite these skirmishes, this road and its forts are visible confirmation of their control of some highland areas.

On this highway, the past oppresses the present in a disconcerting muddle of images, bringing you to the reality of the events and motives of the people who constructed it. This is no vague history lesson. To stand on this road is to feel the motion of those who passed by. Take the time to pause awhile, and you might sense the ghosts of the people who made the journey along this mountain, their voices ringing out a strange foreign language; a people who brought this land into a new phase of history.

Like any lone traveller who passed this way, it is often the case that you come upon some unexpected and misshapen mound, stopping to wonder at this curiosity with its encircling ditch. A little further, the ground to your left or right suddenly disappears into a deep conical depression. Further along the track, a large grey shape appears, only to disappear again as the mist drifts across your field of view. It is difficult to quell the unease these surrounding invoke as you struggle to make some sense of the scene. Ever fearful of an attack by the fearsome tribes whose reputation for ferocity were legend, you hurry your steps desperate to reach the safety of the small intermediate fort which has been recently constructed near the crest. Despite the long campaigns that quelled most of the uprisings in this area, there are always bands of opportunists who lie in wait for a lone traveller! Suddenly, a dark shape materialises out of the smoke grey fog and your fears rise in a stomach surging wave of anxiety. Then, in a brief moment the cloud clears and you gasp, partly in surprise, partly in relief, as the dark stranger is revealed to be a memorial stone known as Maen Madog. Examine the ancient Latin text, and you will read.

DERVAC FILIVS IVST HIC IACIT
(The stone) of Dervacus, son of Justus. He lies here).

Like that Roman, you soon realise that you are just one of many people who, down the centuries, have left their mark on this landscape, whether it be in the form of some megalithic monument, a stone circle, pillow mound, or a well trodden Roman road. These mountains and valleys, like the rock on which they are founded, are of old stock and even though there may be little record to tell of the ancient people who passed this way, the very landscape shouts it out.

Grid Ref: SO 915155
Sarn Helen

Following the directions at the end of Chapter One, return to the point where you parked the car at Pont Cwm Pwll-y-rhyd. From this point walk across the bridge and follow the path to a stile. Cross the stile and continue following the path, which turns right and ascends through a wooded area. This will eventually join the route of the ancient Roman road at the top of the rise. Follow the road to the right, over several other stiles, heading down towards the river in the valley to your right. On reaching the valley bottom, cross the ford (water levels permitting) and ascend the opposite slopes. Halfway up, the road reveals its ancient foundations in the stone surface laid down by its Roman builders. Continuing onwards, we reach *Maen Madog*, an ancient memorial stone bearing Latin inscription.

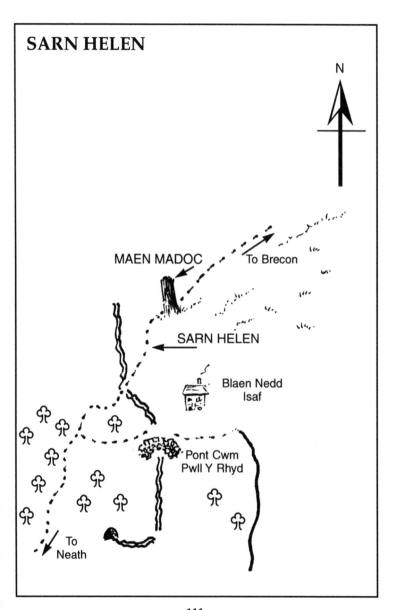

SARN HELEN

MAEN MADOC
To Brecon
SARN HELEN
Blaen Nedd Isaf
Pont Cwm Pwll Y Rhyd
To Neath

Carreg Cennen Castle

Chapter Eleven

Celt and Castles

This stage of our journey takes us through an area that for me is a personal favourite, Y Mynydd Du *(The Black Mountain)*. This is a wild and remote place having a quality that could easily be the setting for some Dark Age legend. This most westerly region of The National Park is the least visited, and officially classified as a wilderness, a ranking that adds to its character and reputation. Here, you can expect to encounter a landscape that, over centuries, has been moulded by Welsh rainfall percolating through soft limestone to scour and shape river gorges and dark valleys.

In his quest for profit, man has also affected the landscape; digging into the mountain in pursuit of the limestone, tearing it from the ground in huge quantities. Unlike nature, he did not seek to heal the wounds. Instead he chose to ravish the land, leaving a legacy of ugly spoil heaps. Nature, however, has come with her healing touch, covering the scars with green balm, setting wild hawthorns amongst the outcrops. She has also created and recreated fascinating and entrancing natural hillocks and rockeries. In the steep sided valleys you will find oak, hazel, and birch cloaked in generous mantles of lichèn, whilst along the riverbanks, lush green mosses and slippery algae seek out every exposed surface.

Anyone taking the time to seek out the haunted and the remote should explore this mountain where they will find timeworn remains that still guard the high places. Roam these hills and you will find *Castell Carreg Cennen*, a beautiful castle that must rank as one of the most haunting and evocative ruins in the whole of Wales. Sitting atop a 300 foot (91m) sheer limestone rock wall in a seemingly impregnable defensive position, its situation within this ancient wilderness imbues it with a magic and mystique evocative of some ancient fable. Here is the home of 'y bwncath' *(the buzzard)*, its plaintive cry heard for miles as it soars high above the castle ramparts in wide and far ranging circles. Some say it carries the lost souls of Welsh achers who are assigned to forever haunt these high places. With this setting in this landscape, it hardly needs a stretch of the imagination to conjure up Myrddin *(Merlin)* from the very stones of the mountain. However, in these hills, the stones have even greater and more ancient tales to tell.

From Castell Carreg Cennen, and some five kilometres to the north-east, a second more ancient defensive construction sits in isolation high above the Dyffryn Tywi. Taking its name from the distinctive autumnal hue of the bracken, which sweeps over its ramparts, 'y Garn Goch', *(the red fort)* is another magnificent example of continuity of purpose and settlement within this area of west Wales. Set in rolling hills some 700 feet (250m) above the southern bank of the Afon Tywi, *y Garn Goch* is a stone walled enclosure covering some 240 acres of land, overlooking the curiously named little hamlet of Bethlehem.

Believed to have been constructed in the early Bronze Age, y Garn Goch served as a settlement site and defensive position during the period 2,000 to 1,400 BC. Here you will find evidence of bronze and Iron Age huts, Iron Age building sites, a pond, cattle enclosures, cairns and other notable features. Over the centuries, this hill fort was extended and consolidated to meet the threats posed by the newly expanding Celtic tribes. However, it was inevitable that with their new Iron technology, weapons and warrior cult, the westward moving Celts would soon come to dominate the native tribes. Some centuries later, the Celts/Brythons/Early Welsh would find themselves within these same walls, probably making their stand against the newly invading Roman legions. It is also possible that the icon of Welsh history, legend and folklore, 'Caratacus' (to the Welsh, *Caradog*), son of the Brython King 'Cunobellinus' *(Cymbeline)* walked within these walls. In his final battle with the Romans, who were led by Ostorius Scapula, Caradog, his wife and daughter, were among many prisoners taken. Caradog eventually escaped and sought protection with the *Brigantes* tribe in the north, led by their queen, *Cartimandua*. His freedom was short lived however when Cartimandua surrendered him to the Romans. He was later taken to Rome in AD 51, where the Emperor Claudius exhibited him in triumph. However, defeat in battle was one thing but humiliation was another. Caradog was not the kind of man allow captivity to suppress his courage, his defiance or his dignity. The Roman historian Tacitus records his defiant speech to his captors in the following terms.

'I had horses, men, arms and wealth. Are you surprised that I am sorry to lose them? If you want to rule the world, does it follow that everyone else welcomes enslavement? If I had surrendered without a blow before being brought before you, neither my downfall nor your victory would have become famous.'

So impressed was Claudius by the dignity and courage of his captive guest that he issued Caradog and his family a full pardon. He died in Rome in AD 54.

Now abandoned, y Garn Goch is a lonely, windswept place. However, as if to reinforce the magic, the aptly named Red Kite, *y Barcud Coch*, now patrols these ancient perimeter walls. I have watched this rare, endangered and beautiful bird dancing on the wind above the rock outcrops and ramparts, forever seeking out the slightest movement from within and near its ancient walls.

Not only does y Garn Goch provide us with the visible history and culture of an ancient people, it also speaks to us of their human condition; of their daily effort to maintain a simple way of life, and of their hopes, motives and fears. The story of

Y Garn Goch

the people who occupied this wildly remote and beautiful location need not be gleaned from some archaic record for it is written in the stones themselves and exudes from the grey and venerable walls of this edifice.

Subdued and silent now, this ancient hill fort remains unbowed, dominating the landscape and watching over Dyffryn Tywi like some old soldier who refuses to drop his guard. Within the National Park you will find many testaments of stone, written by an ancient people. Y Garn Goch is such an example; a proud, defiant sentinel of a forgotten age. By stubbornly refusing to surrender to the inevitable judgement of history, y Garn Goch and Castell Carreg Cennen have once again taken up arms against new foes of climate and time. May they long continue the battle, thereby providing inspiration to artists and romantics alike.

Grid Ref: SN 668194 & SN 690244
Castles and Celts

Returning to the A4969, which runs between Brynaman and Llangadog, we head for the car park just beneath the summit, which offers spectacular views across the patchwork quilted fields of mid and west Wales. From here we start the descent towards Llangadog, and on negotiating the first sharp right hand bend that we come to, we look out for a narrow unmade road on our left. Take this road, following it through the unusual landscape until we descend into a narrow valley. Follow the road signs for Trapp and continue along the route until we eventually see signposts for Carreg Cennen Castle. Follow the signs to the site.

After leaving the castle, we retrace our route until we come to a crossroads. Here we follow the signs for Bethlehem. Eventually the road will take us to the foot of *y Garn Goch*.

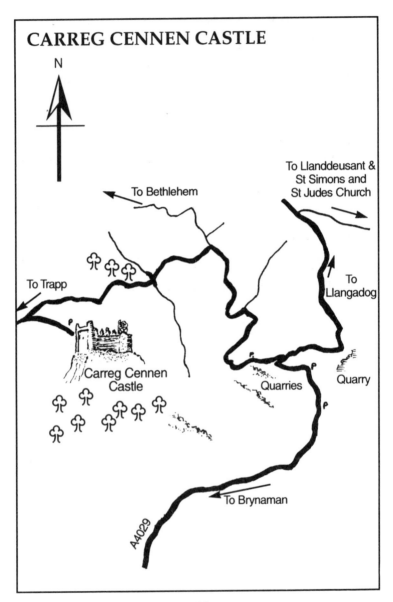

CARREG CENNEN CASTLE

N

To Bethlehem

To Llanddeusant &
St Simons and
St Judes Church

To Trapp

To Llangadog

Carreg Cennen
Castle

Quarries

Quarry

To Brynaman

A4029

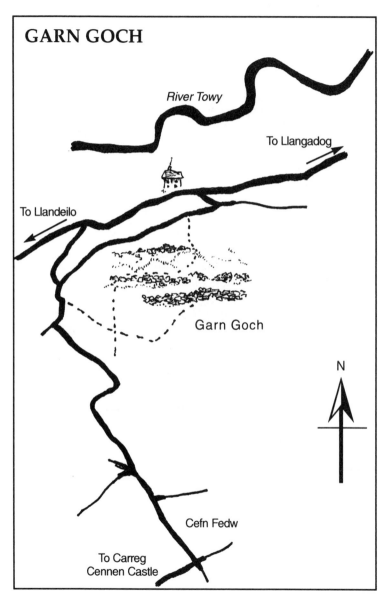

GARN GOCH

River Towy

To Llangadog

To Llandeilo

Garn Goch

N

Cefn Fedw

To Carreg
Cennen Castle

*St. Simon and St. Jude's Church,
Llanddeusant*

Chapter Twelve

Celt to Christian

En route to our final sacred place, the motorist can get some appreciation of the splendour of this beautiful area by taking the A4069, which climbs from the village of Brynaman towards the little town of Llangadog. After travelling up through the foothills, you begin the opposing descent where you will no doubt pull into the little car park just beyond the brow of the hill. From here you can view the canvas upon which man, and nature, have expressed themselves. Before you, in sprawling splendour, is the undulating patchwork quilt landscape of Llangadog and Llandeilo.

Follow the road down, and you will soon enter a deeply wooded glen where Afon Sawdde races down from its source high in the hills. Crossing this young river we head eastward towards the tiny hamlet of Llanddeusant where, beneath the imposing heights of Bannau Sir Gaer the shy little church of St Simon and St Jude rests in anonymous and isolated antiquity.

To the casual observer this could easily be just another unsurprisingly weather worn ecclesiastical building, so typical of these remote and beautiful mountain settlements. The present day structure is said to date from the fourteenth century, whilst the oak beamed barrel ceiling was added in the fifteenth. Due to its remote situation this little church escaped the attention and subsequent ravages of religious reform instigated by Henry VIII, later pursued and consolidated by his son, Edward VI. Consequently, it now claims – almost self consciously – to be the only church in the County having possession of a 1525 pre reformation silver paten. But our interest in this little church lies not in the recent past, but to a period immediately following the demise of Roman influence and military presence within the Islands.

It was in these mountains that Christianity continued to develop in the faith handed down by the early church 'fathers'. Nowadays, a somewhat fashionable view has arisen that this surviving remnant of the early church was a separate and distinct branch of Christianity, and that an established and self identifiable 'Celtic' church reflected a separate institutional structure in that it rejected its Roman origins. It is a notion that seems attractive amongst many well-meaning and deeply spiritual people, but a notion that I fear owes more to wishful thinking than established fact. Indeed, all the evidence points otherwise, and anyone taking the time to pursue an open and honest examination of the facts will see that this so called 'Celtic Church' owes its distinction not to some fanciful notion of early Christian schism, but to its particular geography, culture, and isolation. Nevertheless, it is important to appreciate that these are arguments of a secular kind. Spirituality does not adopt secular values. Let us continue in the position we have adopted and not look on this little church as representing dogmatic principles. See instead the inspiration that drove the doctrine. Let us not fall into the trap of allowing the doctrine to drive the spirituality.

It was this spirituality that inspired those early Welsh/Celtic holy men and women, or *Saints* as they came to be called, to seek out the remote desert places where they sought to express their love of God. In the tradition of the monastic ideal they wandered these hills and mountain meadows, living in isolation and marking out their cell or hermitage as a *Llan*, an ancient word that loosely describes a place of enclosure. Gradually, their simple holiness and way of life attracted like-minded souls and monastic communities were to spring up around these *Llannau*. Soon communities became hamlets, which began villages and occasionally towns. The legacy of these early Christian settlements are still to be seen in Wales. They are usually reflected in the place names of the founding father – Llandeilo *(St Teilo)*, Llan-giwg *(St Ciwg*, although the English spelling of *Llanguicke* is most confusing), and many others including Llansteffan, Llanfrynach, Llangadog, etc.

Long after the saint had died, the enclosure continued to be the focus for religious ceremony and worship and several ancient churches can be found today standing within or near the remains of the original *Llan*. Such enclosures were usually oval or circular in shape, and when seen enclosing a church usually give some indication of the antiquity of the site. But it is not only the existence of a *Llan* in a place name that confirms a town's spiritual pedigree. Very often, the social and cultural practices expressed in village folk festivals and fairs can identify a community's association with particular customs and ideas. In such festivals, it is often the case that a particular saint is honoured, and the date of the festival corresponds to that saint's anniversary.

Llanddeusant celebrates two saints in its name, the annual fair being on 10 October. The two disciples, St Simon and St Jude, both pillars of the early Christian Church, receive the honours of dedication, confirmed by the fact that these two saints both celebrated their anniversaries in October. However, why is the date of the annual fair on the 10th of the month, whilst the anniversary date of the two saints is 28 October! Now there may be other explanations for this anomaly, but consider for a moment the words of a venerable father of the early church; a man that we should perhaps turn for an explanation of the origins of this little community and its sacred site. The following is taken from *Lives of the Welsh Saints* by G H Doble.

'Having received his master's blessing and kiss of peace, and leave to depart, he went forth and sought the seclusion of a certain desert place which adjoined his father possessions. There he built some cells and a little oratory, which they say, is now a monastic settlement containing numerous buildings bearing the names of his two brothers already mentioned. Here he received from the Bishop the dignity of the priesthood, and lived for some time with twelve presbyters who desired to obey his precepts in everything relating to the monastic life.'

The above extract was written by a St Wrmonoc, a monk from Brittany who, in 884, wrote an account of the actions of a brother monk, St Paulinus, who left his community in Llantwit Major to live in solitude 'serving God in the uninterrupted life of contemplation'.

Earlier in his work, Wrnomoc identifies the two brothers as Potolius and Notolius who, with Paulinus, were three of ten children of King Glywys. In *Lives Of The Welsh Saints* G H Doble goes on to satisfactorily prove that the site of this early monastic settlement is indeed Llanddeusant. The evidence for this assumption is adequately supported when we recall that the date of the village fair was 10 October, which happens to be the anniversary of a St Paulinus! It would seem likely that whilst the later church building may be dedicated to more notable pillars of the Christian faith, the very foundations were laid, quite literally, by St Paulinus sometime prior to 650AD.

In the entrance porch of another, similar little church, that of St Michael's at Llanfihangel, Talyllyn just outside Brecon, there stands a large stone pillar. No one can tell how this cigar shaped monolith came to be embraced within this building. It is believed that, like St Simon and St Jude at Llanddeusant, this building stands upon Christian foundations that were laid sometime during the seventh century. An examination of the stone reveals that an unusual hollow has been sculpted at the top. You will remember the ancient biblical text concerning the stones being anointed with oil and water (Chapter 4: *The Megalith*). Is this stone an echo of that practice? Is the hollow in the top of the stone intended to hold a liquid? Alternatively, could there be another, more intriguing explanation?

Whilst I maintain that the Celtic Church was a response to a relatively recent 'Christian' doctrine, brought to this country by missionaries of the Roman Church, I somehow feel that when the structure of this 'new' Christianity was put into place, it sometimes literally stood upon foundations that were considerably more ancient. Whilst pondering on the possibility of spiritual continuity between this little church and what has gone before, I am instantly thrust into a realisation that the parallels may be even more ancient. Throughout Wales and Ireland, there is ample evidence to suggest that the early church 'fathers' often absorbed the stone monoliths of the old pagan religions into their buildings, for they can often be found forming part of the exterior walls or even the fabric of the church itself. At Llanfihangel, the church of St Michael's is said to stand on the foundations of an ancient Pagan temple! Could the modification of this primitive monolith and the siting of the church be a ritual act of 'sanctification', or an absorption of the old order into the new 'Christianity? Looking again at the stone, it is not difficult to imagine that this venerable rock found a new role. With the religious practices of the ancient ways in decline, and the influx of a new order in these mountains, it wasn't too long before the sacred site upon which it stood became the focus for new ideas. Having remained undisturbed for thousands of years and it's sacred role assured, the ancient craftsman's tools would soon chisel out the socket where the wooden cross of Christianity would be mounted to create a symbol of the new religion. It was, to put it simply, another step on the long journey towards truth.

Returning to St Simon's and St Jude's and standing within the enclosure of this little church, I cannot help but reflect on the majesty and mystery of my surroundings. Raising my eyes to the imposing heights of Bannau Sir Gaer and Bannau Brycheiniog, I once again see the dark amphitheatre walls that embrace the dark waters of Llyn y Fan Fach. Conscious of the sacred nature of these hills, one cannot fail to be aware of an overpowering sense of spiritual continuity that has permeated these mountains.

Is it not possible that, when Paulinus first traced out the oval boundary of his *Llan* at Llanddeusant, he was echoing the actions of his Bronze Age ancestors who had marked out Cerrig Duon, only some six kilometres away? Is it not more feasible that this site already contained a stone circle, which Paulinus absorbed into his Christian enclosure, building his cell or hermitage within it and thereby sanctifying this pagan site in the name of Christianity? Are not the roots of an ancient and primitive spirituality grounded here? Is this not a spirituality that was first expressed in the stone megalith of Maen Lia, and later developed and expanded in the oval setting of Cerrig Duon, to be transmuted into the stone pillar at Llanfihangel, Talyllyn and now absorbed into a 'Christian' spirituality?

> *'From one single stock he not only created the whole human race so that they could occupy the entire earth, but he decreed how long each nation should flourish and what the boundaries of its territory should be. And he did this so that all nations might seek the deity and, **by feeling their way towards him, succeed in finding him.**' Acts Ch 17: V 26:29.*

Grid Ref: SN: 777246
Celts and Christians

For directions to this site, see the directions given at the end of Chapter Nine headed 'Dark Depths,' relating to the route through Llanddeusant. St Simon and St Jude's church lies on the route to the lake.

ST SIMON & ST JUDES PARISH CHURCH LLANDDEUSANT

St Simon & St Jude

Hostel

To Cross Inn

To Llyn y Fan

To Llangadog

Afon Sawdoe

Addendum.

Every year, thousands of people tramp their determined way around the 'Brecon Beacons National Park.' However, the park's peaks and slopes are not to be taken lightly. Many visitors, including fit and healthy soldiers who regularly train in these hills, have lost their lives. Should a trek be considered, then in the interest of safety the relevant Ordnance Survey route maps should be used. I have included rough sketch maps of the sites in question, but these are intended for basic route planning only, for they are hand drawn and not to scale. These, and the accompanying directions are based on the Ordnance Survey Maps for grid areas SN and SO. It must be said that anyone who wishes to walk these mountains should be familiar with map and compass before setting out. The need for adequate clothing and refreshment on any walk into the hills is of major importance.

You will notice that the locations and sites that are highlighted in these chapters do not follow a logical route. This is because we are visiting the sites in order of age and evolution. The relevant grid references are included should you wish to plan a tour of the sites in accordance with your own particular needs. Whilst we are mainly concerned with ancient landscapes and prehistoric structures, it would be churlish to exclude other notable sites of antiquity that may not fall within the category of prehistoric, but are of great interest to ramblers, romantics and dreamers alike. With this in mind, I am sure you will forgive the occasional detour to view a scene or structure from a relatively more recent past.

Finally, this book does not purport to be an academic study, and neither is it a work of reference or reasoned argument. However, I have included a limited bibliography for further research should the reader require.

Bibliography

Sir John Rhys. *Celtic Folklore. Welsh & Manx.* Oxford University Press. 1901.

Doble, G H, *Lives Of The Welsh Saints.* University of Wales Press. 1971.

Royal Commission on Ancient And Historical Monuments In Wales.
Mynydd Du and Fforest Fawr. The Evolution of an Upland Landscape.

Evans, Wade. *Parochiale Wallicanum.* 1911.

Davies, John, *A History Of Wales.*

WALKING AND MOUNTAINEERING

- ## WALKS ON THE LLŶN PENINSULA
  PART 1 – SOUTH & WEST – N. Burras & J. Stiff. This series combines walks with history, stories and leg ends. Pastoral walks as well as coastal & mountain panoramas.
  ISBN 0-86381-343-7; £4.50

- ## WALKS ON THE LLŶN PENINSULA
  PART 2 – NORTH & EAST – N. Burras & J. Stiff. *ISBN 0-86381-365-8; £4.50*

- ## WALKS IN THE SNOWDONIA MOUNTAINS
  - Don Hinson. 45 walks, mostly circular, 96 pages, inc. accurate maps and drawings. 96pp.
  ISBN 0-86381-385-2; Revised edition; £3.75

- ## WALKS IN NORTH SNOWDONIA
  - Don Hinson. 100km of paths to help those wishing to explore the area further. 96pp.
  ISBN 0-86381-386-0; Revised edition; £3.75

- ## NEW WALKS IN SNOWDONIA
  - Don Hinson. 43 circular walks together with many variations. This book introduces you to lesser known paths and places which guide book writers seem to have neglected. Maps with every walk. Pen & ink drawings. 96pp. *ISBN 0-86381-390-9; Revised edition; £3.75*

- ## CIRCULAR WALKS IN NORTH PEMBROKESHIRE
  - Paul Williams, 14 walks, 112 pages. *ISBN 0-86381-420-4; £4.50*

- ## CIRCULAR WALKS IN SOUTH PEMBROKESHIRE
  - Paul Willams, 14 walks, 120 pages. *ISBN 0-86381-421-2; £4.50*

- ## FROM MOUNTAIN TOPS TO VALLEY FLOORS
  - Salter & Worral. Detailed information for casual/family walks and for the more adventurous walker.
  ISBN 0-86381-430-1; £4.50

- ## CIRCULAR WALKS IN THE BRECON BEACONS NATIONAL PARK
  ISBN 0-86381-476-X; £4.50

- ## CIRCULAR WALKS ON ANGLESEY
  22 walks by Dorothy Hamilton *ISBN 0-86381-478-6; £4.50*

- ## CIRCULAR WALKS IN GOWER
  14 walks by Nick Jenkins *ISBN 0-86381-479-4; £4.50*

- ## CIRCULAR WALKS IN CENTRAL WALES
  14 walks by Stephen Edwards *ISBN 0-86381-480-8; £4.50*

- ## CIRCULAR WALKS IN GWENT
  15 waks by Richard Sale *ISBN 0-86381-477-8; £4.50*

- ## THE LAKES OF ERYRI
  - Geraint Roberts. Wildlife, fishing and folklore enhances this book aimed at anyone who loves Snowdonia. PVC cover; 256 pp. *ISBN 0-86381-338-0; £8.90*

- ## THE MOUNTAIN WALKER'S GUIDE TO WALES
  - Colin Adams. A comprehensive guide to 100 routes covering 200 Welsh peaks. 192 pp.
  ISBN 0-86381-154-X; Map, PVC cover; £6.90

- ## THE BOTANISTS AND GUIDES OF SNOWDONIA
  - Dewi Jones. An account of the local guides and the plant hunters. 172 pp. *ISBN 0-86381-383-6; £6.95*

- ## WALKS FROM LLANDUDNO
  - Christopher Draper. *ISBN 0-86381-559-6; £4.95*

- ## CIRCULAR WALKS IN MEIRIONNYDD
  - Dorothy Hamilton. *ISBN 0-86381-545-6; £4.50*

- ## WALKS IN AND AROUND THE BERWYN MOUNTAINS
  - John Tranter. *ISBN 0-86381-547-2; £4.50*

WELSH HISTORY/PEOPLE

PEMBROKESHIRE AND CARMARTHENSHIRE

- **CIRCULAR WALKS IN NORTH PEMBROKESHIRE**
  - Paul Williams, 14 walks, 112 pages. *ISBN 0-86381-420-4; £4.50*

- **CIRCULAR WALKS IN SOUTH PEMBROKESHIRE**
  - Paul Williams, 14 walks, 120 pages. *ISBN 0-86381-421-2; £4.50*

- **THE STORY OF PEMBROKESHIRE**
  100 pp. *ISBN 0-86381-253-8; £3.75*

- **THE SLATE QUARRIES OF PEMBROKESHIRE**
  - Alun John Richards. Including illustrations & maps. *ISBN 0-86381-484-0; £3.50*

- **THE LAUGHARNE POEMS**
  - Thomas Crowe. Poems by the first writer since Dylan Thomas to work from the boat house.
  ISBN 0-86381-432-8; £4.50

CENTRAL WALES

- **CIRCULAR WALKS IN MEIRIONNYDD**
  - Dorothy Hamilton. *ISBN 0-86381-545-6; £4.50*

- **THE MEIRIONNYDD'S STORY**
  - Michael Senior; 64 pp; full of illustrations. *ISBN 0-86381-442-5; £1.95*

- **WALKS IN AND AROUND THE BERWYN MOUNTAINS**
  - John Tranter. *ISBN 0-86381-547-2; £4.50*

- **CIRCULAR WALKS IN CENTRAL WALES**
  ISBN 0-86381-480-8; £4.50

- **WALKS IN THE WYE VALLEY**
  - Richard Sale. *ISBN 0-86381-555-3; £4.50*

- **CIRCULAR WALKS IN THE BRECON BEACONS NATIONAL PARK**
  ISBN 0-86381-476-X; £4.50

- **SLATE QUARRYING IN CORRIS**
  - Alun John Richards. First detailed account of the area. 144 pp. *ISBN 0-86381-279-1; £5.45*

- **BOTH SIDES OF THE BORDER**
  An Anthology of writing on the Welsh Border Region by Dewi Roberts.
  ISBN 0-86381-461-1; £4.75

- **A STUDY OF RADNORSHIRE PLACE-NAMES**
  - Richard Morgan. 96 pp. *ISBN 0-86381-475-1; £4.50*

- **A STUDY OF BRECONSHIRE PLACE-NAMES**
  - Richard Morgan, R.F. Peter Powell. *ISBN 0-86381-567-7; £4.50*

- **Rhosydd - A Personal View/Golwg Bersonol**
  Quarry photographs by Jean Napier. *ISBN 0-86381-470-0; £8.95*

- **THE STORY OF BRECKNOCK**
  - Wendy Hughes; 104pp. *ISBN 0-86381-316-X; £4.25*

- **RADNORSHIRE - A HISTORICAL GUIDE**
  - Donald Gregory. *ISBN 0-86381-284-8; £4.50*